SPIRIT

IN THE

NEW TESTAMENT

T0345954

SPIRIT

IN THE

NEW TESTAMENT

AN ENQUIRY INTO THE USE OF THE WORD ΠΝΕΥΜΑ
IN ALL PASSAGES, AND A SURVEY OF THE
EVIDENCE CONCERNING

THE HOLY SPIRIT

BY

EDWARD WILLIAM WINSTANLEY, B.D.

Trinity College, Cambridge
Inspector of Religious Education in the Diocese of Lichfield

CAMBRIDGE :

at the University Press

1908

CAMBRIDGE UNIVERSITY PRESS
Cambridge, New York, Melbourne, Madrid, Cape Town,
Singapore, São Paulo, Delhi, Tokyo, Mexico City

Cambridge University Press
The Edinburgh Building, Cambridge CB2 8RU, UK

Published in the United States of America by
Cambridge University Press, New York

www.cambridge.org
Information on this title: www.cambridge.org/9781107600249

© Cambridge University Press 1908

First published 1908
First paperback edition 2011

A catalogue record for this publication is available from the British Library

ISBN 978-1-107-60024-9 Paperback

PREFATORY NOTE.

THE following little work is the result of a personal study of the original sources, as far as they were attainable to the writer, carried on during the past few years in very broken and far-separated periods of leisure. The author felt the need himself of some synopsis of all the passages relating to 'spirit' in the N.T., and has endeavoured to supply it: this forms Part I. The material therein gathered may be of some service to others. Also with reference to those passages alluding to the divine Spirit and His influence, the author has sought to apprehend the general teaching of the N.T. literature: this forms Part II.

The views therein contained claim no authority save as those of a humble searcher, who has at least desired to work ἐν πνεύματι ἁγίῳ.

The writer expresses his cordial thanks to Dr Swete, Professor Barnett, and Canon Allison, for their kind help in revising the proofs.

E. W. W.

ROOSENDAAL,
   WOLVERHAMPTON,
     January 1908.

CONTENTS.

BOOKS USED FOR REFERENCES.

The New Testament in the Original Greek.—WESTCOTT AND HORT.

The Old Testament in Greek according to the Septuagint.—SWETE. (3 vols.)

And, for other literature,

Die Apokryphen und Pseudepigraphen des Alten Testaments.—KAUTZSCH. (2 vols.)

Neutestamentliche Apokryphen.—HENNECKE.

Patrum Apostolicorum Opera.—GEBHARDT-HARNACK-ZAHN.

INTRODUCTORY SURVEY.

BEFORE setting forth the references in which the word πνεῦμα occurs in the writings of Apostolic days, it seems fitting to afford a cursory glance of its use in the Greek Old Testament, and this covers to a very large extent that of its Hebrew original רוּחַ. If we may, to allow for textual uncertainty, put the number of instances at approximately 343, we find that only about nine times is any other word than רוּחַ so translated in the LXX., and there are roundly six occasions when it is not represented at all in the Massoretic text. Speaking broadly, therefore, our inquiry into the use in the LXX. gives us a very general idea of the various manners in which, from the prophetic age to the Christian era, the Jews regarded the Spirit of God or the spirit of man. Although following on a somewhat lengthy survey of the literature, this brief chapter is only set down tentatively to indicate some distinctions which we have found to be useful.

We can group the writings roughly as

1. Canonical, (a) pre-exilic, (b) post-exilic, and
2. Extra-canonical. But we are quite unable to draw any hard and fast lines, because some of the references may be regarded as belonging either to (a) or (b), according to the critical position with respect to a particular

passage or verse: all that can be done is to make generalizations to serve for guidance.

Keeping in view the acknowledged fact that the tribal or national is the more prominent feature in early religion, and that among the Jews it is only when we reach Jeremiah and Ezekiel that the individual as such comes to have a clearly personal religious value, we classify the references to the divine Spirit as related to the nation, the individual, and the world: while as regards the nation further sub-division becomes convenient according as those who are God's instruments for the fulfilment of His purposes therein are judges, kings, prophets, Messiah etc., and passages referring to the Spirit and the individual as such will either be external and occasional, or more internal, ethical, and continuous in effect.

Following upon these, it is needful to set forth a few examples of various meanings relating to the spirit of man in these periods, but in this case any subdividing or grouping such as the spirit as the sphere of emotion or of volition, or as representative of the whole personality, must be dependent on the standpoint of the reader in many instances, and therefore ill-defined and elastic.

Some references with 'evil' connotation are also supplied.

1. Canonical Literature.

(a) *Pre-Exilic.*

Divine Spirit.

A. In Nation. Through

i. Judge. Ju. vi. 34, xiii. 25, xiv. 6, 19, xv. 14 (warlike and heroic deeds).

ii. King. 1 Regn. x. 6, 10, xi. 6, xix. 20, 23 (Saul's mantic), xvi. 13 (David).

iii.   Prophet.   3 R. xviii. 12, 4 R. ii. 9, 15, 16 (Elijah and Elisha stories, external, violent impulse), ? Mic. iii. 8 (internal endowment), also patriarchal-prophetic Gen. xli. 38 (Joseph).

[Compare *evil* spirit from God on kings, 1 R. xvi. 14 —23, xviii. 10 (A), xix. 9 (Saul), 4 R. xix. 7 (Sennacherib): on prophets, 3 R. xxii. 21–3, Mic. ii. 11 ?, ? Is. xix. 14 (Egypt), (cf. xxx. 1).]

B.   In Man.

1.   Occasional (prophetic, ecstatic), see A, in that the individuals influenced are of public rather than personal importance.

2.   Permanent (inward, ethical), Is. xi. 2 (cf. xxxii. 15), yet even the Messianic character is valued nationally more than individually.

C.   In World.

No certain early references available.

Human spirit.

Higher aspect of human nature, virtually identical with soul.

(*a*)   emotional, 3 R. xx. 5, cf. Gen. xli. 8 ψ., (of strength or weakness) Gen. xlv. 27, Josh. ii. 11, Ju. xv. 19, 1 R. xxx. 12, 3 R. x. 5 (E.V.).

(*b*)   volitional, Dt. ii. 30 (ἐσκλήρυνεν).

(*c*)   personal, apparently no early instance.

1.   (*b*)   *Post-Exilic.*

Divine Spirit.

A.   In Nation.

Little trace of any but iii., of prophetic endowment in the coming (Messianic) time, Is. xliv. 3, Joel ii. 28 f., or in the past, Zech. (i. 6), vii. 12, Hag. ii. 5, Neh. ix. 20, 30.

Also, in Priestly narratives, of characters closely connected
with cult or government of old: Ex. xxxi. 3, xxxv. 31
(Bezalel), Nu. xi. 17, 29 ff., xxvii. 18, Dt. xxxiv. 9
(Moses and Joshua).

B. In Man.

1. Occasional, very frequent in Ezekiel, ii. 2, iii. 24
(ἦλθεν), iii. 12, 14, viii. 3, xi. 1, 24, xliii. 5 (ἀνέλαβεν),
xi. 5 (ἔπεσεν), xxxvii.; also Dan. v. 12, vi. 3, 1 Ch. xii.
18, xxviii. 12, 2 Ch. xv. 1, xx. 14, xxiv. 20, all more or less
ecstatic or prophetic.

2. Ethical, (a) Ps. l. 12, 13 (τὸ πνεῦμα τὸ ἅγιόν σου),
14, cxlii. 10 (τ. π. σου τὸ ἅγιον, v.l. ἀγαθόν, cf. Neh.
ix. 20). Zech. xii. 10 (π. χάριτος καὶ οἰκτιρμοῦ). Ez.
xi. 19, xviii. 31, xxxvi. 26 f. (all π. καινόν ‖ καρδία).
(b) More specially of the guidance of the best, the
'Servant' etc., for purposes of salvation. Is. xxxii. 15 ?,
xxxiv. 16, xlii. 1, xliv. 3, lix. 21, lxi. 1 ?, Zech. iv. 6.

In such instances the language at least is of individuals,
whether the interpretation be congregational or Messianic.

C. In World.

In Creation and created life, Gen. i. 2, (vi. 3), vi. 17,
vii. 15 (P.), Ps. xxxii. 6, ciii. 30, Job xxvii. 3, xxxiii. 4 (π.
θεῖον), Is. xlii. 5, lvii. 16 (‖ πνοή), Zech. xii. 1, Ecc. xii. 7
(returning to God).

Tending to hypostasis, Is. xlviii. 16 ?, lxiii. 10 (παρώξυναν τὸ πνεῦμα τὸ ἅγιον αὐτοῦ), 11, 14, Ps. cxxxviii. 7,
cf. Ez. i. 21, x. 17 (π. ζωῆς in vision of God) ?

Spirit-beings ? Ps. ciii. 4 (but Heb. 'winds').

[Evil implication, Zech. xiii. 2 (ἀκάθαρτον).]

Frequently in the literal meaning of wind, breath, and
also figuratively of vanity (esp. Ecc.).

Human spirit.

(a) emotional, Ps. lxxvi. 4, cv. 33, cxli. 4, cxlii. 4, 7, Pr. xv. 4 (v.l. πιότητος), Is. lxv. 14, Ecc. vii. 10, x. 4, Job xxxii. 18, Ez. xxi. 7, Dan. ii. 3, x. 8, 17 (וְהוֹדִי and נִשְׁמָה?), iii. 39 (∥ ψυχή).

(b) volitional, Jahweh ἐξήγειρεν Pul, Tiglath-Pileser, Cyrus, Zerubbabel, etc. (1, 2 Ch., Ezra, Jer.).

Rather of disposition, Ps. xxxiii. 19, l. 19, lxxvii. 8.

(c) personal, Ps. xxx. 6, lxxv. 13, ciii. 29, cxlv. 4, Job x. 12, Ecc. iii. 21 (iii. 19 and Job xxxiv. 14 perhaps better under C). Ez. iii. 14, xi. 5 (rational).

2. EXTRA-CANONICAL.

Divine Spirit.

A. In Nation. Few references, and only in and through Messiah (looking forward). Enoch xlix. 3 (wisdom), lxii. 2 (righteousness), Ps. Sol. xvii. 42 (holiness), xviii. 8 (wisdom, righteousness, etc.), Test. Levi xviii. (holiness), Judah xxiv. (of holy Father, of grace, etc., cf. Arm. of truth).

B. In Man.

1. Occasional—(mostly of old-time heroes) ecstatic, Enoch lxxi. 5, 11, xci. 1 (outpoured ∥ word), prophetic, Jub. xxxi. 12 (Isaac), xxv. 14 (Rebekah), xl. 5 (Joseph), Sus. 45 (Dan. v. 12, vi. 3), Ecclus. xlviii. 24 (Isaiah), Test. Levi ii., 4 Ezr. v. 22, cf. Sib. iii. 701, cf. 817.

2. Quasi-permanent, and ethical—Sus. 62, En. lxi. 11 (angel virtues), Test. Sim. iv., Judah xx., Naph. x. (Heb.), Benj. iv., viii., cf. Wisd. i. 5 (quasi-personified), vii. 7, ix. 17 (τ. ἅγ. σου π.), Ecclus. xxxix. 6, mostly of understanding and the like.

C. In World.

God is conceived more transcendentally, and is not in direct contact with matter. Still the Spirit is source of created life Jud. xvi. 14, Ap. Bar. xxi. 4 quasi-personified ‖ voice or word, yet pervades rather than creates the universe (Wisd. i. 7, xii. 1): but there are created spirits of natural phenomena En. lx. 12 ff., Jub. ii. 2. Spirit-beings abound in later speculation as ministerial agencies, e.g. 'Lord of spirits' in Enoch over 100 times, Jub. x. 3 (God of spirits), 2 Macc. iii. 24, of angels and men, cf. Jub. xv. 31 f. over nations. God's Spirit tends to be hypostatized, Wisd. i. 7, ix. 17, xii. 1, inherent in Wisdom, or even identified therewith vii. 22 (A om. ἐν).

[With an evil connotation; often of fallen angels, Enoch xiii. 6, xv. ff., lxvii. 8 f.: more generally, Tob. vi. 8, Jub. vii. 27, xi. 4, En. xv. 8 f., Ps. Sol. viii. 15 (π. πλανήσεως).]

πνεῦμα of wind etc. frequently.

Human spirit.

Sphere of emotion, En. lx. 4.

More generally, of highest part of man, personal life separable at death and persisting, Ecclus. xxxi. 14, xxxviii. 23, Tob. iii. 6, Bar. ii. 17, Jub. xxiii. 31, Jud. x. 13 (man = π. ζωῆς), Enoch xli. 8, lxxi. 1, xcviii. 10, ciii., cviii.

It may be noted that in Enoch πνεῦμα and ψυχή are both used of existence after death, the (separable) π. being the narrower term; while only ψυχή appears En. ix. 3, xxxvi. 4, lxiii. 10 ?, cii. 5, 11, ciii. 7, cf. Ap. Bar. xxx. 2, 4, and so with 4 Ezr. vii. 32 ('souls' for judgement, but vii. 78 'spirit' separable from body, qu. Ecc. xii. 7), so also vii. 85, 93, 99, 100; but also πνεῦμα of the dead En. ix. 10 'spirits of souls,' xvi. 1 'spirits out of the souls of their flesh,' xxii. 3 seemingly, 'spirits of the souls of the dead,' xxii. 5 probably, 'I saw the spirit of a dead man' etc. Cf. Dan. iii. 86 'spirits and souls.'

In Wisdom, π. and ψ. are used in parallel clauses xv. 11, xvi. 14 of life inbreathed by and rendered to God, but πνεῦμα only xv. 16, cf. Jub. xii. 3, 5, 2 Macc. vii. 22 f., xiv. 46 ?

Ps. Sol., again, only have ψυχή.

Such examples as are here collected are at least sufficient to indicate a gradual progress, in dealing with the Spirit of or from God, towards the intellectual, ethical and more permanent in effect, within post-exilic and extra-canonical writings: on the human side towards more developed and more definite usage in different portions of the literature. All direct action seems to cease to be attributed to the divine Spirit in cosmic life (except in the book of Wisdom), and in national life (except in so far as regards the anticipated Messiah). The later Jews looked back on the idealized past while bemoaning the comparative absence of the Spirit's work in their own days (only Bath Kol etc.): and God in His majestic glory was too holy, too pure, too afar off, to have direct dealing with man and the world of nature, Wisdom and ministerial spirit-beings must bridge the space between. The gleam of hope that came from the prophetic word— and was not the Spirit of prophecy the Author ?—that in and through Messiah this Spirit would act upon men in richer mode and wider diffusion than before, prepared the way for the N.T. experiences.

Preliminary.

After this slight survey of usage in O.T. and other Jewish literature, we can now address ourselves to the examination of the N.T. data.

The Second Gospel, as a whole, being now generally accepted as the earliest written record in Gospel form that we possess, and at the least estimate more than three-quarters thereof being incorporated—with literary adjustments, amplification of detail, re-arrangement of material—in the other two Synoptists' narratives, it seems but natural to give the references contained therein the first place, rather than those from the Gospel which has the foremost position in our printed texts, and bears Matthew's name.

The writers and books are referred to in as brief a manner as is consistent with clearness, and, in the Gospel passages, where the usage is identical and the references are directly parallel, such reference is indicated by a single or double asterisk, that immediately next to the number implying a parallel in Matthew (M.), and that further to the right of it one in Luke (L.).

For those few references that are common to M. and L., a dagger marks the fact in the same place.

For quotations from the Scriptures of the Old Testament incorporated in any passages uncial characters are used.

Also, for the sake of convenience, wherever the words or the context imply 'evil' spirit or spirits, the occurrences are enclosed in square brackets.

PART I.

§ 1. SYNOPTISTS.

S. Mark.

1**. i. 8 ἐγὼ ἐβάπτισα ὑμᾶς ὕδατι, αὐτὸς δὲ βαπτίσει ὑμᾶς πνεύματι ἁγίῳ.

M. iii. 11 ἐγὼ μὲν ὑμᾶς βαπτίζω ἐν ὕδατι εἰς μετά-νοιαν...αὐτὸς ὑμᾶς βαπτίσει ἐν πνεύματι ἁγίῳ καὶ πυρί.

L. iii. 16 ἐγὼ μὲν ὕδατι βαπτίζω ὑμᾶς...αὐτὸς ὑμᾶς βαπτίσει ἐν πνεύματι ἁγίῳ καὶ πυρί.

πνεῦμα ἅγιον is here conceived as the influence or power coming from God through Messiah upon men, of which the baptism of John with water is but a prefiguring.

The invisible is contrasted with the visible, the vehicle of spiritual cleansing with the material of physical cleansing. The ἐν added by M. and L. (also before ὕδατι in M.) makes no real difference to the sense, the ideas of element and instrument shade into one another here.

The addition of καὶ πυρί in M. and L. is somewhat difficult to explain with certainty: in both Syr. Sin. implies καὶ πυρί first; may not the original tradition have been one in which ὕδατι was balanced by πυρί, fire of cleansing or of Messianic judgement on the unrighteous (cf. context and Enoch lxiii. 10, etc.), and primitive Christian experience tended to combine the saying with the Pentecostal interpretation thereof, cf. Ac. ii. 3.

In Enoch, Ps. Sol., Test. XII. Patr., Messiah both possesses πνεῦμα ἅγιον, רוח הקדש רוח קדשא, as the ancient worthies of the race for occasional purposes, only he possesses the endowment in its ideal completeness, and also (Test. Levi xviii., Jud. xxiv., etc.) dispenses it to others.

2**. i. 10 εἶδεν σχιζομένους τοὺς οὐρανοὺς καὶ τὸ πνεῦμα ὡς περιστερὰν καταβαῖνον εἰς αὐτόν.

M. iii. 16 καὶ ἰδοὺ ἠνεῴχθησαν οἱ οὐρανοί, καὶ εἶδεν πνεῦμα θεοῦ καταβαῖνον ὡσεὶ περιστερὰν ἐρχόμενον ἐπʼ αὐτόν.

L. iii. 22 (ἐγένετο)...ἀνεῳχθῆναι τὸν οὐρανὸν καὶ καταβῆναι τὸ πνεῦμα τὸ ἅγιον σωματικῷ εἴδει ὡς περιστερὰν ἐπʼ αὐτόν.

It seems hardly possible to doubt that these three expressions here used by the Synoptists mean ultimately the same, for all connect the special presence with the 'anointing' of the Baptism. The Marcan article takes up *v.* 8, the spirit by which and in which Messiah was to baptize was his to dispense, for it came on him to remain (εἰς), or it may mark a personification of God's Spirit, though not quite in the same manner as that of Wisdom or Word (Reason) in later Alexandrian (Jewish) thought.

πνεῦμα θεοῦ, only here in Synoptists. Five times in Ro., 1, 2 Cor.: τ. π. θεοῦ or τ. π. τοῦ θεοῦ, however, once in M., 4 times in 1 Cor., in 1 J. once, and in 1 P. τὸ τοῦ θεοῦ πνεῦμα. In Gosp. Hebrews it is the Holy Spirit who speaks, like the Shekinah (Tg. Ex. xxiii. 15, xxiv. 9), and it is also to Jesus Himself only, calling Him 'her first-born son.'

τὸ πνεῦμα τὸ ἅγιον is a very favourite Lucan expression, 20 times in G. and Ac., and only 10 times in the rest of the N.T. (11 if Eph. iv. 30 τ. π. τ. ἁ. τοῦ θεοῦ be included). Here the

MSS. shew how M.'s π. θεοῦ soon became in transmission the fuller and more definite τὸ π. τοῦ θεοῦ.

Mark regards the vision as primarily a manifestation to and experience of our Lord Himself, while in 'John' it is for the Baptist's recognition of the Messiah.

3**. i. 12 καὶ εὐθὺς τὸ πνεῦμα αὐτὸν ἐκβάλλει εἰς τὴν ἔρημον.

M. iv. 1 τότε ὁ Ἰησοῦς ἀνήχθη εἰς τὴν ἔρημον ὑπὸ τοῦ πνεύματος.

L. iv. 1 καὶ ἤγετο ἐν τῷ πνεύματι ἐν τῇ ἐρήμῳ.

From the Baptism and its attendant vision onwards Mark's story regards Jesus as under the continual influence and direction of the divine Spirit, and for his readers τὸ πνεῦμα was already sufficiently definite and intelligible without qualification. M. softens ἐκβάλλει into ἀνήχθη, which is also geographically correct, while he expresses the agency (ὑπό) of the divine guidance, as L. does rather the sphere (ἐν, though the use of the preposition has become very indeterminate), and he adds two allusions to this guidance here and 14. In Gosp. Heb. (frag. 1) the 'Source of all holy spirit' descends, and (frag. 2) 'my mother the Holy Spirit seized me,' cf. Ezekiel's record of his experience, viii. 3, and Bel 36; while for the violence of spiritual impulse cf. Enoch frequently, also Ac. viii. 39, etc.

For the desert as the abode of demons, cf. Nu. xvi. 22, Tob. viii. 3, M. xii. 43, Berachoth 3, etc. It is noteworthy that in Gosp. Heb. Mt Tabor is the scene, that (traditionally) of the Transfiguration; may this point to a duplicate tradition of the manner in which Jesus related His Temptation?

[**4** *. i. 23 καὶ εὐθὺς ἦν ἐν τῇ συναγωγῇ αὐτῶν ἄνθρωπος ἐν πνεύματι ἀκαθάρτῳ.

L. iv. 33 καὶ ἐν τῇ συναγωγῇ ἦν ἄνθρωπος ἔχων πνεῦμα δαιμονίου ἀκαθάρτου.]

This time of the sphere of control of an evil (unclean) spiritual influence, cf. v. 2. It is not necessary here to investigate the belief in 'demonic possession' as the cause of disease, and, especially, nervous disorders, suffice it to admit that it was widespread and firmly held by all classes, and that Jesus apparently accepted these opinions of His time. We may contrast the divine control, M. xxii. 43, 1 Cor. xii. 3, Apoc. i. 10, etc.

It is also deserving of remark that a more technical phrasing is used by L. the first time 'evil' spirit occurs : the genitive seems to be of apposition (cf. v. 1. δαιμόνιον ἀκάθαρτον). Justin, too, uses δαίμονες, not πνεύματα.

[5. i. 26 καὶ σπαράξαν αὐτὸν τὸ πνεῦμα τὸ ἀκα-θαρτον...ἐξῆλθεν.

Cf. L. iv. 35 καὶ ῥίψαν αὐτὸν τὸ δαιμόνιον...ἐξῆλθεν.]

τ. π. τ. ἀκαθ. taking up 23.

σπαράσσειν, only ix. 20 (συν-), 26, and L. ix. 39 otherwise in N.T. L. keeps his more definite δαιμόνιον alone.

[6 *. i. 27 κατ' ἐξουσίαν καὶ τοῖς πνεύμασι τοῖς ἀκαθάρτοις ἐπιτάσσει.

L. iv. 36 ὅτι ἐν ἐξουσίᾳ καὶ δυνάμει ἐπιτάσσει τοῖς ἀκαθάρτοις πνεύμασιν.]

Mk expresses vividly the popular generalization, whether from this act alone, or from many of which he selects this one sample. L. frequently affords us the physician's sense not only of power delegated, but also of power manifested (καὶ δυνάμει), and the touch is peculiar to him (cf. similar sense in Mk v. 30). ἐπιτάσσειν, else Mk thrice, L. thrice, Ac. xxiii. 2, Phlm. 8.

7. ii. 8 καὶ εὐθὺς ἐπιγνοὺς ὁ Ἰησοῦς τῷ πνεύματι αὐτοῦ....

Cf. M. ix. 4 καὶ εἰδὼς ὁ Ἰησοῦς....

Cf. L. v. 22 ἐπιγνοὺς δὲ ὁ Ἰησοῦς....

The first time that this usage of τὸ π. as the human spirit, man in his inmost being, confronts us; hardly to be distinguished from ἐν ἑαυτῷ, cf. J. xi. 33.

ἐπιγνούς, the compound here only in Mk and L. To both later compilers τῷ π. αὐτοῦ seems needless: perhaps from motives of reverence, cf. Mk viii. 12 with M. xvi. 2, etc.

[**8** *. iii. 11 καὶ τὰ πνεύματα τὰ ἀκάθαρτα, ὅταν αὐτὸν ἐθεώρουν, προσέπιπτον αὐτῷ,...

(Cf. M. xii. 15 κ. ἐθεράπευσεν αὐτοὺς πάντας.)

L. vi. 18 καὶ οἱ ἐνοχλούμενοι ἀπὸ πνευμάτων ἀκαθάρτων ἐθεραπεύοντο.]

Cf. i. 23, 26, 27 for morbid manifestations, such as epilepsy, ascribed popularly to 'evil' spirits or demons. M. affords a brief summary only, but heightens the effect (πάντας), cf. change in M. viii. 16. L.'s passage must be treated as parallel, though he alters the previous verses to suit his setting, and makes stylistic and technical improvements on Mk. In view of v. 17, and of viii. 43 (ἀπ' οὐδενὸς θεραπευθῆναι), ἀπό here goes better with ἐνοχλ., illustrating its increasing usage to mark agency.

θεραπεύειν, only Ac. 5 times, J. v. 10, Ap. xiii. 3, 12, outside Synn. (Mk 6, M. 16, L. 14).

9* *. iii. 29 ὃς δ' ἂν βλασφημήσῃ εἰς τὸ πνεῦμα τὸ ἅγιον, οὐκ ἔχει ἄφεσιν εἰς τὸν αἰῶνα.

M. xii. 31 ἡ δὲ τοῦ πνεύματος βλασφημία οὐκ ἀφεθήσεται.

L. xii. 10 τῷ δὲ εἰς τὸ ἅγιον πνεῦμα βλασφημήσαντι οὐκ ἀφεθήσεται.

Is it incautious to regard the 'blasphemy' as, in the first instance, ascribing to 'evil' influence, the spirit of Beelzebul, what is manifestly from 'good' influence, the πνεῦμα θεοῦ, רוח קדשא, of whose operation in and through Him Jesus is supremely conscious? A presence so objectively realized as in the Baptism-vision renders 'blasphemy' in reference to the manifestation in Christ's activity equivalent to irreverent speech in reference to the ultimate source, God Himself, and is thus contrasted with speaking evil of the human instrument. The truly religious cannot fail to distinguish the source of Jesus' beneficent power, but wilful perversity precludes repentance and so forgiveness. M., we shall see, extends and yet limits the original application.

Possibly we may compare Enoch xx. 6, though that passage itself is uncertain in its interpretation.

[**10.** iii. 30 ὅτι ἔλεγον Πνεῦμα ἀκάθαρτον ἔχει.]

Seemingly an editorial touch, recalling the mind to the charge of v. 22, possibly not original.

We are led to compare the charge (δαιμόνιον ἔχειν) and answer found in J. viii. 48 ff.

[**11.** v. 2 εὐθὺς ὑπήντησεν αὐτῷ ἐκ τῶν μνημείων ἄνθρωπος ἐν πνεύματι ἀκαθάρτῳ.]

Cf. M. viii. 28 ...ὑπήντησαν αὐτῷ δύο δαιμονιζόμενοι ἐκ τῶν μνημείων ἐξερχόμενοι.

Cf. L. viii. 27 ...ὑπήντησεν ἀνήρ τις ἐκ τῆς πόλεως ἔχων δαιμόνια.]

Similar to the use in i. 23, only of 'evil' (unclean) control. L. in his way improves the expression, again using δαιμόνιον. M.'s narrative tends to shew us how the details of a story became varied in the course of transmission, or, possibly, how two instances of the cure of a 'possessed' were combined.

[**12** *. v. 8 ἔλεγεν γὰρ αὐτῷ Ἔξελθε τὸ πνεῦμα τὸ ἀκάθαρτον ἐκ τοῦ ἀνθρώπου.

L. viii. 29 παρήγγελλεν γὰρ τῷ πνεύματι τῷ ἀκαθάρτῳ ἐξελθεῖν ἀπὸ τοῦ ἀνθρώπου.]

The command is implied in M. viii. 31 f.

τ. π. τ. ἀκ. as in Mk 7 times, L. twice, altogether: not at all in M. in the full form. The nominative with article takes the place of the little used vocative. L. phrases it better, and uses again for the more broken but more vivid ἔλεγεν κ. τ. λ., παρήγγελλεν, v. 14, viii. 56, ix. 21 and 11 times in Ac.: also his favourite ἀπό, in constr. with ἐξέρχεσθαι. Here the impf. (though there is a v.l. aor.) need not be pressed.

[13. v. 13 καὶ ἐξελθόντα τὰ πνεύματα τὰ ἀκάθαρτα εἰσῆλθον εἰς τοὺς χοίρους.

Cf. M. viii. 32 οἱ δὲ (δαίμονες) ἐξελθόντες ἀπῆλθαν εἰς τοὺς χοίρους.

Cf. L. viii. 33 ἐξελθόντα δὲ τὰ δαιμόνια ἀπὸ τοῦ ἀνθρώπου εἰσῆλθον εἰς τοὺς χοίρους.]

τὸ πνεῦμα, v. 8, where the 'possessing' spirits are identified with the man, who speaks for himself (με, 7) though giving his name as 'Legion' (9): perhaps also the transference to the swine influenced the number in 13. To M. the usual need to know the 'name' does not hold for Jesus. L. has again δαιμόνιον and ἀπό, though viii. 29 τ. π. τ. ἀκ. after δαιμ. 27.

[14*. vi. 7 καὶ ἐδίδου αὐτοῖς ἐξουσίαν τῶν πνευμάτων τῶν ἀκαθάρτων.

M. x. 1 ...ἔδωκεν αὐτοῖς ἐξουσίαν πνευμάτων ἀκαθάρτων.

Cf. L. ix. 1 ...ἔδωκεν αὐτοῖς δύναμιν καὶ ἐξουσίαν ἐπὶ παντὰ τὰ δαιμόνια.]

The fuller form τ. π. τ. ἀκ. as v. 13.

The genitive is objective, anarthrous in M., who generalizes and expands, increasing the effect (ὥστε ἐκβάλλειν αὐτὰ κ. θεραπεύειν πᾶσαν νόσον κ. πᾶσαν μαλακίαν). L.'s changes are instructive, he inserts δύναμις, as in iv. 36, only this time before ἐξουσία, he improves the constr. (ἐπί), and also adds a heightening touch to his oft-used δαιμόνια to cover all forms of 'possession' (πάντα).

[15. vii. 25 ἧς εἶχεν τὸ θυγάτριον αὐτῆς πνεῦμα ἀκάθαρτον.

Cf. M. xv. 22 ἡ θυγάτηρ μου κακῶς δαιμονίζεται.]

θυγάτριον, v. 23, Mk only.

δαιμονίζεσθαι, cf. v. 2 above, where M. again uses the vb

(M. 7 times, Mk four, L. viii. 36, J. x. 21 in N.T.). Here M. sets the story differently, and alters the more detailed tradition of Mk, probably that Jesus should not quit the Holy Land. One may doubt if the story was ever contained in the second source of M. and L., for surely L. would have retained it.

16. viii. 12 καὶ ἀναστενάξας τῷ πνεύματι αὐτοῦ λέγει....

As in ii. 8, where sphere of knowledge, also with αὐτοῦ, the inmost part represents the personality, the self : as the highest aspect of the human nature perhaps regarded as especially the scene of operation of the πν. θεοῦ. Increasing reverence for the Master seems to have eliminated (in M. xvi. 1) this lifelike touch, as in vii. 34 (here the whole story is solely Marcan). The 'groanings' in S. John are apparently of doctrinal significance (xi. 33, xiii. 21, where ταράσσω is used, ἀναστ. here only). Conversely, the hum. spirit experiences joy, L. i. 47 (x. 21).

[**17** *. ix. 17 Διδάσκαλε, ἤνεγκα τὸν υἱόν μου πρὸς σέ, ἔχοντα πνεῦμα ἄλαλον.

Cf. M. xvii. 15 Κύριε, ἐλέησόν μου τὸν υἱόν, ὅτι σεληνιάζεται καὶ κακῶς ἔχει.

L. ix. (38) 39 Διδάσκαλε, δέομαί σου ἐπιβλέψαι ἐπὶ τὸν υἱόν μου, ὅτι μονογενής μοί ἐστιν, καὶ ἰδοὺ πνεῦμα λαμβάνει αὐτόν.]

L. has simply π., as cause of seizure, but τὸ δαιμ. v. 42. πν. ἄλ. cf. v. 25 below, also somewhat similar vii. 32, cf. L. xi. 14 (δαιμ...κωφόν). For the interchange of victim and 'spirit' or 'spirits' influencing him, cf. v. 2 ff.

L.'s sympathy with disease—e.g. (μονογενής) bringing grief to the home, the power of the eye in such cases (ἐπιβλέψαι) and the description of the symptoms (39 f.)—is prominent. σεληνιάζεσθαι, M. only, also iv. 24, late.

[**18**. ix. 20 καὶ ἰδὼν αὐτὸν τὸ πνεῦμα εὐθὺς συνεσπάραξεν αὐτόν.

Cf. L. ix. 42 ἔτι δὲ προσερχομένου αὐτοῦ ἔρρηξεν αὐτὸν τὸ δαιμόνιον καὶ συνεσπάραξεν.]

τὸ πνεῦμα, taking up the π. ἄλαλον, 17.

The sufferer and the cause are identified, the personal 'spirit' and the personal victim, cf. v. 9 f., unless Syr. Sin. be correct in implying the omission of ὁ παῖς, as subject of ἰδών. L. again introduces δαιμόνιον, and though retaining the comp. συνεσπάραξεν (only here), places before it the more expressive ἔρρηξεν. Possibly L. avoids the colloquial σπαράσσω by itself, as (39) he combines it with μετὰ ἀφροῦ, while iv. 35 he replaces σπαράξαν by ῥίψαν. M. omits both these details, and the discussion: Jesus had no need to make inquiries (M. xvii. 17).

[**19** *, **20**. ix. 25 ἐπετίμησεν τῷ πνεύματι τῷ ἀκαθάρτῳ λέγων αὐτῷ Τὸ ἄλαλον καὶ κωφὸν πνεῦμα.

Cf. M. xvii. 18 καὶ ἐπετίμησεν αὐτῷ ὁ Ἰησοῦς.

L. ix. 42 ἐπετίμησεν δὲ ὁ Ἰησοῦς τῷ πνεύματι τῷ ἀκαθάρτῳ.]

For the address of command τὸ ἄλ. κ. κωφὸν π. cf. v. 8, also 41 (cf. Aram. stat. absol., and Heb. with art.), yet ix. 19, all Synoptists have ὦ.

ἐπιτιμᾶν only in Synn. (M. seven times, Mk nine, L. twelve) and 2 Ti. iv. 2, Ju. 9.

21*. xii. 36 αὐτὸς Δαυεὶδ εἶπεν ἐν τῷ πνεύματι τῷ ἁγίῳ....

M. xxii. 43 ...Δαυεὶδ ἐν πνεύματι καλεῖ αὐτὸν κύριον....

Cf. L. xx. 42 αὐτὸς γὰρ Δαυεὶδ λέγει ἐν βίβλῳ ψαλμῶν....

God's power filling, inspiring men of old to word and act tends in later days to become hypostatized, cf. Dan. v. 12,

vi. 3, Sus. 45 ⊙., Jud. xvi. 14, Wisd. i. 5, 7, vii. 22, ix. 17, xii. 1, Test. Jud. xx., xxiv., Syr. Bar. xxi. 4, Jub. xxv. 14, etc., though never ultimately identified with God in nature, but only as energizing, in operation. In Talmudic passages אמרה רוח הקדש is used of Scripture, though it is conceived as distinct from God; 'in' it the prophets spoke, cf. the words ascribed to the Spirit Ac. iv. 25, xxviii. 25, unlike the vaguer undefined רוח of the O.T., of which speaking is not recorded. Further, in early Christian extra-canonical writings, cf. 1 Clem. xiii. 1, xvi. 2, xxii. 1, xlv. 2, etc., all τ. π. τ. ἅ.; Barn. vi. 14, ix. 2, of prophets, τ. π. Κυρίου; of Abraham and Moses ix. 7, x. 2, 9, ἐν πνεύματι; Did. xi. 7, 8, 9, 12 of Christian prophets, ἐν π.

ἐν βίβλῳ L. only (except Phil. iv. 3) iii. 4, Ac. i. 20, vii. 42, explanatory for Gentile readers.

22. xiii. 11 οὐ γάρ ἐστε ὑμεῖς οἱ λαλοῦντες ἀλλὰ τὸ πνεῦμα τὸ ἅγιον.

Cf. M. x. 20 οὐ γὰρ ὑμεῖς ἐστὲ οἱ λαλοῦντες ἀλλὰ τὸ πνεῦμα τοῦ πατρὸς ὑμῶν τὸ λαλοῦν ἐν ὑμῖν.

Cf. L. xii. 12 τὸ γὰρ ἅγιον πνεῦμα διδάξει ὑμᾶς ἐν αὐτῇ τῇ ὥρᾳ....

but in ‖ L. xxi. 15 ἐγὼ γὰρ δώσω ὑμῖν στόμα καὶ σοφίαν, the power ascribed in Mk to τ. π. τ. ἅ., in M. to τ. π. τοῦ πατρός, is yet Christ's own to dispense, cf. Ac. ii. 33, Ps. Sol. xviii. 8, Test. Judah xxiv., Levi xviii.

The power of speech in days of persecution comes from God, as with Hebrew prophetic characters, and Christian prophets afterwards (Ap. xix. 10). In such use 'the Holy Spirit' is almost a periphrasis for the Holy Name, though the later Jews conceived of רוח הקדש as distinct from God, cf. Tg. Onk. Gen. i. 2 רוחא מן קדם יי. So the Shekinah is used to avoid God's name, and is parallel with the Spirit, having wings likewise (Sota 13, Sabb. 31 A, Sanhed. 96 B), cf. Mk i. 10, and spoke, or sounded, as medium of inspiration (Tg. Ex. xxxiii. 3, 15, etc. in anthropomorphic passages). Here where the Spirit is an objective reality distinct from Jesus and the Father, the Jewish hypostatization may not be disregarded. The Lucan ‖ reminds of J. xv. 26, xiv. 26 of witness to the glorified Christ, guided by the 'Paraclete,' though not as in this instance occasional. For the Spirit teaching, cf. Sus. 44, 45, Bereshith R. 85, etc.

23*. xiv. 38 τὸ μὲν πνεῦμα πρόθυμον, ἡ δὲ σὰρξ ἀσθενής.

M. xxvi. 41 identical.

For the first time π. directly contrasted with σάρξ in N.T. as different aspects of human personality. The highest in man, the πνεῦμα, rational and volitional, channel of the divine π.'s activity, and like ψυχή surviving death, is set over against the lower nature, the σάρξ, which man possesses in common with the animals, cf. Gen. vi. 17. In Synn. no expression seems to imply a trichotomy (cf. M. x. 28, it is ψ. persists, and is God's alone to destroy, if He will, this man can but do to the σῶμα). In (the Alexandrian) Wisd. soul and spirit interchange, the former, as in M., contrasted with body i. 4, viii. 19 f., ix. 15 (‖ νοῦς), the latter also = soul in its highest aspect, xv. 8, 16 (ψ. life = π. breath from God), xvi. 14 (ψ. and π. in ‖ στίχοι).

S. Matthew.

We next examine occurrences of the word πνεῦμα in M. that have not been already treated as direct parallels to the Marcan passages. By reason of the independence of the Birth stories, references therein are dealt with separately.

24. i. 18 εὑρέθη ἐν γαστρὶ ἔχουσα ἐκ πνεύματος ἁγίου.

This ἐκ π. ἁ., to define the divine source of the Babe's earthly life, only meets us here and v. 20 in N.T. We may compare Ignatius' statement, Eph. xviii. 2 ὁ γὰρ θεὸς ἡμῶν

Ἰ. ὁ Χ. ἐκυοφορήθη ὑπὸ Μαρίας κατ' οἰκονομίαν θεοῦ ἐκ σπέρματος μὲν Δαβίδ, πνεύματος δὲ ἁγίου.

25. i. 20 τὸ γὰρ ἐν αὐτῇ γεννηθὲν ἐκ πνεύματός ἐστιν ἁγίου.

As v. 18 above. π. in both cases anarthrous, as very commonly after preposition. Conceptive power rather than personification seems intended, if the story arose on Palestinian soil, cf. the double gender of רוח, and Gosp. Hebr.'s ἄρτι ἔλαβέ με ἡ μήτηρ μου, τὸ ἅγιον πνεῦμα. Cf. L. i. 35.

26. v. 3 μακάριοι οἱ πτωχοὶ τῷ πνεύματι.

Cf. L. vi. 20 μακάριοι οἱ πτωχοί.

For many reasons, which cannot be considered here, we venture to think that L.'s Sermon fragments are, in the main, more original : the Christian community is not so obviously in the background. τῷ πν. seems a later touch, cf. Ps. xxxiii. 19, the עֲנָוִים, like the disciples, might be literally poor, but also poor 'in spirit,' humble in oppression, lowly in penitence. π. the highest aspect of human nature, the inmost self, whence the springs of character issue in word and deed : in M. only here and xxvi. 41, contrasted with ἡ σάρξ. Compare Is. lxvi. 2 (Heb.).

[**27.** viii. 16 καὶ ἐξέβαλεν τὰ πνεύματα λόγῳ.

Cf. Mk i. 34 καὶ δαιμόνια πολλὰ ἐξέβαλεν....

Cf. L. iv. 41 ἐξήρχετο δὲ καὶ δαιμόνια ἀπὸ πολλῶν....]

M.'s first mention of 'evil spirits,' he generalizes τὰ π. simply, and heightens the effect (λόγῳ), cf. 8, such the Master did not—and need not—touch. L. is characteristic again with δὲ καί, ἐξήρχετο ἀπό.

28. x. 20 οὐ γὰρ ὑμεῖς ἐστὲ οἱ λαλοῦντες ἀλλὰ τὸ πνεῦμα τοῦ πατρὸς ὑμῶν τὸ λαλοῦν ἐν ὑμῖν.

The disciples share the Messianic endowment, Test. Jud. xxiv. Cf Mk. xiii. 11, L. xii. 12. In annotating the former, we did not regard these words as an exact parallel, because, though they are so similar, there is a rearrangement of material. The

enabling power in days of stress will be virtually God Himself
in operation through His Spirit in the disciples, and this seems
in keeping with the later avoidance by many circumlocutions
of the divine Name, and also of God's immediate contact with
life's episodes, to guard His transcendence. The definition
τοῦ πατρὸς ὑμῶν is distinctly Matthaean, reminding of the
Jewish אבינו שבשמים: and in Matthew this Fatherhood of
God appears more than twice as often as in Mk + L. (about
44 to 5 + 16).

29. xii. 18   θήϲω τὸ πνεῦμά μου ἐπ᾽ αὐτόν.

One of M.'s 'testimonia' from the Scripture (the 9th) : he
takes the (proph.) pf. as fut., while LXX. tr. Is. xlii. 1 literally
(ἔδωκα).

30. xii. 28 εἰ δὲ ἐν πνεύματι θεοῦ ἐγὼ ἐκβάλλω
τὰ δαιμόνια.

Cf. L. xi. 20 εἰ δὲ ἐν δακτύλῳ θεοῦ [ἐγὼ] ἐκβάλλω
τὰ δαιμόνια.

M. here, as often, seems more sensitive to anthropomorphism
than the Greek-trained L. π. θεοῦ, in M. only in this place
and iii. 16 (baptismal anointing), not in L., cf. Ac. viii. 39.
Gen. of origin or source is possibly more fitting than the
possessive. The expression, if original, is unique : would not
L., with his manifest fondness for the Spirit's agency, have
kept it ? L.'s ἐν δακτύλῳ is more Jewish (Exod. viii. 19,
Dt. ix. 10, Ps. viii. 4) and preferable (cf. Ac. vii. 50).

31. xii. 32 ὃς δ᾽ ἂν εἴπῃ κατὰ τοῦ πνεύματος τοῦ
ἁγίου....

Cf. Mk iii. 29 n. 'M. extends and yet limits the application,' for the sin is unforgiven in both worlds (οὔτε ἐν τούτῳ
τῷ αἰῶνι οὔτε ἐν τῷ μέλλοντι), while in this additional verse it
is the Christ, as the Son of Man, that is distinguished from
'men' (31) which is M.'s rendering for the unique, if true to
Aramaic original, τοῖς υἱοῖς τῶν ἀνθρώπων of Mk. In L. also,
'men' the instruments do not appear, the contrast is only

between blasphemy (εἰς) against Jesus and against τὸ ἅγιον πνεῦμα. In both M. and L. it seems that the mind of the Church after Pentecost has been moulding the form of the tradition; this seems confirmed by L. xii. 12, the only other place where he uses τ. ἄγ. π.

[**32†**. xii. 43 ὅταν δὲ τὸ ἀκάθαρτον πνεῦμα ἐξέλθῃ ἀπὸ τοῦ ἀνθρώπου....]

L. xi. 24 identical (omitting δέ).

This is in material belonging to the common source ('Logia') of M. and L.—only, while L. links it closely with the Beelzebul story, M. places the 'sign' illustrations (Nineveh's penitence, the Queen of the South's hearing) between, and L. further reverses their order, and omits, if it be original, the 3 days' sign. τὸ ἀκ. π., so only in this verse in M. : L. has it in ‖ and (pl.) iv. 36. M. points the allusion to the Jews (v. 45). For the current belief as to the home of evil spirits, cf. Mk i. 12 n.

[**33†**. xii. 45 τότε πορεύεται καὶ παραλαμβάνει μεθ' ἑαυτοῦ ἑπτὰ ἕτερα πνεύματα πονηρότερα ἑαυτοῦ.

L. xi. 26 τότε πορεύεται καὶ παραλαμβάνει ἕτερα πνεύματα πονηρότερα ἑαυτοῦ ἑπτά.]

L. strikes out the unnecessary μεθ' ἑαυτοῦ and improves the order (ἑπτά last).

π. πονηρότερα ἑ. only in this passage.

(ἀπὸ) π. πονηρῶν occurs L. vii. 21, viii. 2. The exorcism followed by worse 'possession' in completeness (ἑπτά) may be a picture of solely negative repentance. For '7,' cf. Jewish angelological speculation, etc., and Ap. ii. 7.

34. xxvii. 50 ὁ δὲ Ἰησοῦς πάλιν κράξας φωνῇ μεγάλῃ ἀφῆκεν τὸ πνεῦμα.

Cf. Mk xv. 37 ὁ δὲ Ἰησοῦς ἀφεὶς φωνὴν μεγάλην ἐξέπνευσεν.

Cf. L. xxiii. 46 καὶ φωνήσας φωνῇ μεγάλῃ ὁ Ἰησοῦς... ἐξέπνευσεν.

ἀφῆκεν τ. π., cf. Ac. vii. 59, Ecclus. xxxviii. 23 (παρακλήθητι ἐν αὐτῷ ἐν ἐξόδῳ πνεύματος αὐτοῦ), Wisd. xvi. 14 (ἐξελθὸν δὲ πνεῦμα οὐκ ἀναστρέφει, οὐδὲ ἀναλύει ψυχὴν παραλημφθεῖσαν), which leads over to the Greek usage ἀφιέναι τὴν ψυχήν (Gen. xxxv. 18).

πνεῦμα, the God-given principle (or breath) of life, cf. Gen. ii. 7, vi. 17, etc., rendered at death (Ecc. xii. 7).

ἐκπνέειν, only in these parallels, and Mk xv. 39, class.

35. xxviii. 19 πορευθέντες οὖν μαθητεύσατε πάντα τὰ ἔθνη, βαπτίζοντες αὐτοὺς εἰς τὸ ὄνομα τοῦ πατρὸς καὶ τοῦ υἱοῦ καὶ τοῦ ἁγίου πνεύματος.

Cf. Did. vii. 1 βαπτίσατε εἰς τὸ ὄνομα κ.τ.λ. ἐν ὕδατι ζῶντι, the first appearance of the formula elsewhere. Acts, Justin, Aphraates, Eusebius form a strong combination against the genuineness of the words, but this is not for discussion here. The formula would doubtless be current in the time of the final form of M., if we may infer from Syr. ps.-Euseb. that that was towards 120 A.D., and the Gospel implied by the Didache seems almost our M.; the probable original form 'in my name' would be assimilated to Church usage. For 'the Name' cf. En. xxxix. 7, xlviii. 2 (Son), etc. But see J. T. S. VI. (Chase).

S. Luke.

As we approach the passages in Luke wherein πνεῦμα is found, we are prepared for a remarkable development, when we have realized that in L.'s work (Gosp. and Acts) π. meets us nearly twice as many times (per no. of pages) as in M. and Mk together (1·85 approximately). Some years back the writer made an investigation of style and vocabulary to see if they lent any weight to theories which would separate chaps. 1, 2, of the Gospel from the rest of the work, and, though taking various chapters in different parts for comparison, he became quite satisfied in his own mind that the opening chapters were *not* later incorporated but were of a piece with the whole, and *by the same author*. The πνεῦμα references in L., apart from those already treated as parallels to M. or Mk, or both, are as follows:

36. i. 15 καὶ πνεύματος ἁγίου πλησθήσεται ἔτι ἐκ κοιλίας μητρὸς αὐτοῦ.

Our first instance brings a new and unique collocation which only L. affords (cf. 41, 67, Ac. ii. 4, iv. 8, 31, ix. 17, xiii. 9) π. ἁ. πλησθῆναι.

The divine influence, power, or gift is contrasted with artificial means to induce excitement or ecstasy. The local colour is from the LXX. (Nu. vi. 3, 1 R. i. 11). The Spirit-outpouring to mark the new age affects those individuals who took part in the preparation for it also.

37. i. 17 καὶ αὐτὸς προσελεύσεται ἐνώπιον αὐτοῦ ἐν πνεύματι καὶ δυνάμει 'Ηλεία.

ἐν π. κ. δυν. may be regarded as one expression, anarthrous after ἐν, meaning with a similarly powerful divine endowment. L.'s use of δύναμις has been noted (iv. 36) in 6 *, where, however, ἐν ἐξουσίᾳ καὶ δυνάμει marks rather the twofold aspect of Jesus' action towards those possessed. πνεῦμα, רוח הקדש, etc., was conceived as bestowed in especial measure on leaders and prophets, operating in them in old time for the sake of the Theocracy, for national guidance, or else, as here, connected with the Messianic age.

38. i. 35 πνεῦμα ἅγιον ἐπελεύσεται ἐπὶ σέ.

π. ἁ. is quite unobjectionable, we find this form over 25 times in L.'s writings: here, as in M., not strictly personal, but the medium of power (here conceptive) from God, as implied with O.T. characters, Sarah, Hannah, etc., cf. ‖ δύναμις ὑψίστου following.

But *v.* 36 continues *v.* 33, and 34, 35 are at least suspicious, e.g. ἐπέρχεσθαι ἐπί: the usage in Ac. i. 8 is not strictly parallel with the sense here, nor does ἐπεί (34) ever occur in L.'s writings, rather ἐπειδή (4 times) with this meaning : but this discussion does not belong to a conspectus of πνεῦμα references.

39. i. 41 καὶ ἐπλήσθη πνεύματος ἁγίου ἡ Ἐλεισάβετ.

Cf. 15. If רוח הקדש was thought to have ceased with the last prophets (cf. 1 Macc. iv. 46, etc.), it was fitting that the forerunner of the new dispensation should be its recipient even from conception.

40. i. 47 καὶ ἠγαλλίασεν τὸ πνεῦμά μου ἐπὶ τῷ θεῷ τῷ σωτῆρί μου.

L. changes the Semitic figures to expressions more suitable to Greek ears (ψυχή and πνεῦμα in the couplet for καρδία and κέρας of the LXX., 1 R. ii. 1). ἀγαλλιᾶν, chiefly Lucan.

σωτήρ, ii. 11, perhaps through LXX. ἐν σωτηρίᾳ σου.

41. i. 67 καὶ Ζαχαρίας ὁ πατὴρ αὐτοῦ ἐπλήσθη πνεύματος ἁγίου, καὶ ἐπροφήτευσεν λέγων....

So also of Elizabeth 41, π. ἅ. impelling to the special words of 'prophetic' utterance following. Both parents of the forerunner must have been 'spiritually' endowed to fulfil their office in the economy of salvation.

42. i. 80 τὸ δὲ παιδίον ηὔξανε καὶ ἐκραταιοῦτο πνεύματι.

αὐξάνειν, intrans., cf. ii. 40, xiii. 19, Ac. vi. 7, vii. 17, xii. 24, xix. 20 of the 'church' or the 'word,' thus mostly Lucan : here sc. σώματι.

κραταιοῦν, only ii. 40 also in Gospp., where T.R. adds πνεύματι.

πνεύματι, here dat. of respect, denoting the higher aspect of His human nature, which is, as usual with the Jews, regarded as dichotomous.

43. ii. 25 καὶ πνεῦμα ἦν ἅγιον ἐπ' αὐτόν.

44. 26 καὶ ἦν αὐτῷ κεχρηματισμένον ὑπὸ τοῦ πνεύματος τοῦ ἁγίου....

45. 27 καὶ ἦλθεν ἐν τῷ πνεύματι εἰς τὸ ἱερόν.

In *v.* 25 the best reading is unique, strictly 'an impulse which was divine' was, or rather came 'upon,' Symeon (ἐπί acc.): cf. Ac. i. 5.

26. For the pf. pass. cf. Heb. viii. 5 καθὼς κεχρημάτισται Μωϋσῆς. ὑπό, for constr. cf. Ac. x. 22, ἐχρηματίσθη ὑπὸ ἀγγέλου ἁγίου, sc. Κορνήλιος. The periphrastic ptc. is quite Lucan; broadly, in G. and Ac. 3 times M. + Mk.

τ. π. τ. ἅ. also iii. 22 (x. 21 ?), Mk thrice, M. once, Ac. 17 times, of the divine agent operative in and through individuals for the good of the Messianic community, here through the human πνεῦμα.

27. ἐν τ. π. as of Jesus in iv. 1 (**3****), the sphere of influence in which the action takes place is distinguished as divine, cf. iv. 14 ἐν τῇ δυνάμει τοῦ π. also of Jesus.

Thus Symeon, participating in the ushering-in of Christ's time, shares the Spirit-endowment that characterizes it.

46. iv. 1 Ἰησοῦς δὲ πλήρης πνεύματος ἁγίου ὑπέστρεψεν ἀπὸ τοῦ Ἰορδάνου.

Only L.; cf. Ac. vi. 3, vii. 55, xi. 24, also similar vi. 5, 8, ix. 36, xiii. 10, xix. 28, akin to the collocation with πλησθῆναι i. 15, etc.

L. thus more emphatically (doubly, cf. 1 *b* (**3****)) links the Temptation and Baptism together ; here we meet with his favourite ὑποστρέφειν (for ἀπό constr. cf. xxiv. 9 ἀ. τοῦ μνημείου). Physical movement from spiritual impulse, Ac. viii. 39, etc.

47. iv. 14 καὶ ὑπέστρεψεν ὁ Ἰησοῦς ἐν τῇ δυνάμει τοῦ πνεύματος εἰς τὴν Γαλιλαίαν.

L. still keeps the illapse before his readers. The gen.

might be apposition—the divine power identical with the
רוח הקדוש in dove form (cf. Targ. for Cant. ii. 12 וקול התור
נשמע בארצנו)—or marking the source of the power.

For the action, see above note.

48.   iv. 18   ΠΝΕ͂ΥΜΑ ΚΥΡΊΟΥ ἐπ᾽ ἐμέ,
as Isa. lxi. 1 LXX.

π. κ. only here in Gospp. and Ac. viii. 39 (v. 9), though so
common in Gk Bible.   The scene may be put forward from
artistic purpose to serve as an opening and to give a specimen
of interpretation, see v. 23, etc.

[**49.**   vii. 21 ἐν ἐκείνῃ τῇ ὥρᾳ ἐθεράπευσεν πολλοὺς
ἀπὸ νόσων καὶ μαστίγων καὶ πνευμάτων πονηρῶν.]

The summary of works of Christ in the presence of
emissaries of the Baptist is inserted here by L. in the 'common source' matter.   In this verse and in viii. 2 only does
L. write πνεύματα πονηρά, cf. Ac. xix. 12, 13, 15, 16.   We do
not seem to have sufficient data to decide what, if any,
distinction he intended to draw between δαιμόνιον, π. ἀκαθ.,
π. πονηρόν.

θεραπ. ἀπό, constr. only in L., v. 15 and viii. 2: the 3
classes appear to form a climax of severity.

[**50.**   viii. 2 καὶ γυναῖκές τινες αἳ ἦσαν τεθεραπευμέναι
ἀπὸ πνευμάτων πονηρῶν....]

From one of L.'s 'special' (women?) sources, perhaps from
personal converse when in Palestine in the entourage of
S. Paul.

The periphrastic ptc. and the constr. (ἀπό, see above) are
also Lucan traits.   It is curious that he only uses π. πον. here
and a few vv. previously, and then in the account of Ephesus
exorcisms (not a 'we' passage).   Does this suggest a connexion,
and a clue?   Daughters of Philip?   Cf. the confused traditions
from Papias and Polycrates, ap. Eus. H. E. iii. 31, 39.

51.   viii. 55 καὶ ἐπέστρεψεν τὸ πνεῦμα αὐτῆς.

The spirit rendered at death (Ecc. xii. 7) is restored to the

child, and that is betokened by, or to the old world is, the
return of breathing. Cf. Gen. ii. 7 πνοὴ ζωῆς, and Jesus'
death, Mk xv. 37 ∥.

ἐπιστρέφειν, abs. Ac. xv. 36, same phrase Ju. xv. 19.

[**52**.　x. 20 πλὴν ἐν τούτῳ μὴ χαίρετε ὅτι τὰ πνεύματα
ὑμῖν ὑποτάσσεται.]

πλήν is greatly predominant in L. (M. 5 times, Mk once
differently).

ὑποτάσσεσθαι, in Gospp. only L. (ii. 51, x. 17), not in Ac.

τὰ πνεύματα, of all phenomena ascribed to demonic possession.　Exorcism is quite secondary, cf. M. vii. 22.

53.　x. 21 ἐν αὐτῇ τῇ ὥρᾳ ἠγαλλιάσατο τῷ πνεύματι
τῷ ἁγίῳ καὶ εἶπεν....

ἐν αὐτ. τ. ὥρᾳ, L.'s mode of time-definition, though ἐκείνῃ
vii. 21.

ἠγαλλιάσατο, cf. i. 47 with τ. π. for subject, perhaps cf.
Ro. xiv. 17.

τῷ π. τῷ ἁγίῳ, unique in this connexion, M. (xi. 25) introduces the like saying with ἀποκριθείς, the comment is the
Evangelist's and undeniably Lucan, cf. introductory formulæ
in Ac.　Though the emphasis is on the divinely inspired
emotion, yet the sphere of joy is the noblest part of His
humanity, cf. J. xi. 33, etc.

54.　xi. 13 πόσῳ μᾶλλον ὁ πατὴρ [ὁ] ἐξ οὐρανοῦ
δώσει πνεῦμα ἅγιον τοῖς αἰτοῦσιν αὐτόν.

We observe L.'s interpretative manner here in so defining
ἀγαθά (M. vii. 11) in accordance with the special prominence
given to πνεῦμα ἅγιον (and its manifestations) through his
works, yet Syr. Sin. implies ἀγαθά here also, and the confusion
in D and O. Lat. precludes certainty as to the autograph.　In
the last discourses in J. the gift is future, and mediated by
the risen Jesus, if not sent by Him.

55. xii. 12 τὸ γὰρ ἅγιον πνεῦμα διδάξει ὑμᾶς....

From xii. 10 we learn that sin in the face of better knowledge is blasphemy against God, whose representative τὸ ἅγ. π. is. Cf. Mk iii. 29, xiii. 11 n.; to the latter this passage is practically ‖, for the dictum here is not really connected with the subject matter of the context, the help is against foes in legal proceedings.

[**56.** xiii. 11 καὶ ἰδοὺ γυνὴ πνεῦμα ἔχουσα ἀσθενείας ἔτη δέκα ὀκτώ.]

π. ἀσθενείας, gen. of definition, cf. Ro. viii. 15 probably in sense of disposition; the method here is not that usually employed for 'possession' (12, 13), but the cause is 'Satan' (16), so the πνεῦμα may be regarded as 'evil.' Here it does not seem to refer, as so often, to mental disease.

57. xxiii. 46 Πάτερ, εἰς χεῖράς coy παρατίθεμαι τὸ πνεῦμά μογ.

Exactly as LXX. (Ps. xxx. 6), with the necessary change to the present tense.

As in O.T. usage, the God-bestowed higher nature which man has, and which, according to later developments of Jewish thought (Ecc. xii. 7, Zech. xii. 1, etc.), persists after death in the keeping of the 'Lord of spirits' (Nu. xxvii. 16, xvi. 22). The extra-canonical usage varies: Enoch, Jub., Tob., Bar. have (mostly) πνεῦμα, while Wisd., Ecclus, 2 Macc., Ap. Bar., 4 Ezr., and Ps. Sol. prefer (generally) ψυχή for the nobler and lasting part of man in their dichotomy. For the fact, cf. M. xxvii. 50, Mk xv. 37 (ἐκπνέειν), the voluntariness is more prominent in J. xix. 30.

58. xxiv. 37 πτοηθέντες δὲ καὶ ἔμφοβοι γενόμενοι ἐδόκουν πνεῦμα θεωρεῖν.

59. 39 ὅτι πνεῦμα σάρκα καὶ ὀστέα οὐκ ἔχει καθὼς ἐμὲ θεωρεῖτε ἔχοντα.

D has φάντασμα, interpreting as if = 'ghost.' Ign. Smyrn.

iii. 2 δαιμόνιον ἀσώματον, if it be a witness of primitive exposition, cf. also Gosp. Hebr., implies rather spiritual, e.g. angelic being, and the context seems to demand this here; cf. also Ac. xxiii. 8.

For πτοηθῆναι, cf. xxi. 9, class. LXX.

ἔμφοβος, only in L.'s books, and Ap. xi. 13.

[78 references in all, including parallel passages.]

§ 2. ACTS.

We turn next to Vol. II. of Luke's work, for we find that 'spirit' is as prominent in Acts also, so that if this book has been termed the 'Gospel of the Spirit,' we might almost entitle the earlier book the 'spiritual Gospel' but for the use of that name already for S. John. Despite the Aramaic colouring of the earlier chapters, the style and vocabulary are Lucan throughout.

79. i. 2 ἐντειλάμενος τοῖς ἀποστόλοις διὰ πνεύματος ἁγίου οὓς ἐξελέξατο.

διὰ π. ἁ. Again iv. 25.

ἐντειλ. Cf. xiii. 47.

ἐξελέξ. Cf. L. vi. 13 of the selection of the Apostles, cf. Ac. xiii. 17. We are taken back in thought to the divine influence which filled John Baptist (L. i. 15), Jesus' mother (i. 35), Elizabeth (i. 41) and Zacharias (i. 67), as well as our Lord Himself in symbolic completeness (L. iii. 22, iv. 1) as Messiah; cf. x. 38, En. xlix. 3, Ps. Sol. xvii. 42, Test. XII. Patr. Jud. xxiv. etc.

80. i. 5 ὑμεῖς δὲ ἐν πνεύματι βαπτισθήσεσθε ἁγίῳ....

Again, quoted by St Peter as a ῥῆμα τοῦ κυρίου, xi. 16. This is the baptism of 'fire' (or of 'holy spirit') which was, in John Baptist's preaching, a mark and function of the Messiah (cf. L. iii. 16); and so, by way of contrast, in the promise of that fulfilment the Risen Christ refers to the 'water' baptism of John. For the position of ἁγίῳ, cf. L. ii. 25.

81. i. 8 ἀλλὰ λήμψεσθε δύναμιν ἐπελθόντος τοῦ ἁγίου πνεύματος ἐφ᾿ ὑμᾶς.

The references in the Lord's utterances in the opening scene of Ac. connect it very closely with the final words of the Gospel (xxiv. 49 τὴν ἐπαγγελίαν τοῦ πατρός μου...ἕως οὗ ἐνδύσησθε ἐξ ὕψους δύναμιν) before that is concluded with the very brief summary of the Ascension.

But here in i. 8 δύναμιν seems to draw all together, the promise of God (τοῦ πατρός) is the power from God (ἐξ ὕψους), and the power consists in the spiritual influence bestowed for the work of witness and manifested in many manners (τ. ἅγ. π.). In the Gospel we have noted L.'s fondness for δύναμις as power from God in action (cf. i. 17, 35, iv. 14, 36, v. 17 (vi. 19), viii. 46, ix. 1 (from Christ)). In Ac., as L. xix. 37, the word is also used of the effect (e.g. ii. 22, viii. 13, xix. 11). Cf. Talm. גבורה of God himself, Sabb. 87 A.

τὸ ἅγιον πνεῦμα also ii. 38 (gift received), iv. 31 (filling men), ix. 31 ('comforting' Church), xiii. 4 (sending men), xvi. 6 (hindering them), thus taking various complexions of meaning with language of greater or less personification.

82. i. 16 ἔδει πληρωθῆναι τὴν γραφὴν ἣν προεῖπεν τὸ πνεῦμα τὸ ἅγιον διὰ στόματος Δαυείδ....

τὸ πνεῦμα τὸ ἅγιον, in this book again ii. 33, v. 3, 32, vii. 51 (Q), x. 44, 45, 47 (fell, gift outpoured, received), xi. 15 (fell), xiii. 2 (spoke), xv. 8 (given), 28 (author of decision), xix. 6 (came upon [after imposition of hands]), xx. 23 (witnesses), 28 (appointed), xxi. 11, xxviii. 25 (speaks, or spoke).

'Holy Spirit' is, even more than in the Gospel, by reason of the subject-matter, gift, atmosphere, and guide in the life of Christian community and individual, and also, as in this passage, is conceived as a reverent equivalent for God in operation, esp. manifested as Author of and Speaker in Holy Writ: cf. the usage of the Rabbins, and of the Apostolic

Fathers in quoting Scripture, e.g. Ep. Clement xiii. λέγει γὰρ
τ. π. τ. ἅ. (identified with Logos, cf. xiii., lvi. φησὶν γὰρ ὁ ἅγιος
λόγος) ; xvi. καθὼς τ. π. τ. ἅ. περὶ αὐτοῦ (Jesus) ἐλάλησεν ; xxii.
καὶ γὰρ αὐτὸς διὰ τοῦ π. τ. ἅ. οὕτως προσκαλεῖται ἡμᾶς (where
αὐτός = Christ through the Psalmist), as well as the N.T.
passages Ac. iv. 25 (David), vii. 51, xxviii. 25 (Isaiah) ; Heb.
iii. 7, ix. 8, x. 15 ; 1 P. i. 11 (as π. Χριστοῦ) ; 2 P. i. 21 (ὑπὸ
π. φερόμενοι).

83, 84. ii. 4 καὶ ἐπλήσθησαν πάντες πνεύματος
ἁγίου,...καθὼς τὸ πνεῦμα ἐδίδου ἀποφθέγγεσθαι αὐτοῖς.

π. ἅ. πλησθῆναι, or similarly, iv. 8, 31, ix. 17, xiii. 9, 52 ;
cf. L. i. 15, 41, 67. Like the Jewish רוח נבואה, it seems best
to regard π. ἅ., as also τ. π. which resumes it later, as the God-
bestowed power, the effect rather than the Person, previously
promised, which 'filled' the recipients, and was manifested
primarily in the ἀποφθέγγεσθαι (only ii. 14, xxvi. 25, as well
in N.T.) consisting of 'glossolaly,' rather the ecstatic uncontrolled utterances of the primitive form of the tradition, than
foreign languages (which ἑτέραις here, and 5 ff., apparently
imply), rendered by the κοινή, the Greek of commerce and
every-day life in Mediterranean lands, an unnecessary ac-
quisition.

85. ii. 17 ἐκχεῶ ἀπὸ τοῦ πνεύματός μου ἐπὶ
πᾶσαν σάρκα.

86. 18 ...ἐν ταῖς ἡμέραις ἐκείναις ἐκχεῶ ἀπὸ
τοῦ πνεύματός μου,
as Joel ii. 28 f.

The 'spirit of prophecy' so largely named by the later
Jews (cf. Just. Ap. I. also) as source of inspiration, which
came of old but on fit vehicles of Jahweh's message, or 'in'
which they spake. The first application was within Israel
(cf. x. 45), if not within Palestine, Siphre Dt. xviii. 15, in
Messiah's days.

Ez. xi. 19 (new spirit), Jer. xxxviii. 33 (law in heart), etc.
are comparable.

87. ii. 33 τῇ δεξιᾷ οὖν τοῦ θεοῦ ὑψωθεὶς τήν τε ἐπαγγελίαν τοῦ πνεύματος τοῦ ἁγίου λαβὼν παρὰ τοῦ πατρὸς ἐξέχεεν τοῦτο....

τοῦτο, sc. the phenomenon of 'tongues' with the accompanying physical manifestations ('seen and heard'), itself regarded as representative of the fulfilment of the promise which Jesus received from (παρά) the Father, and a function of the Messiah to possess, and to outpour. (Ps. Sol. xvii. 42, xviii. 8; Test. Levi xviii.; Judah xxiv.)

λαμβάνειν παρά, with gen. Cf. also iii. 5, xvii. 9, xx. 24, xxvi. 10.

ὑψωθείς, cf. v. 31, τῇ δεξιᾷ being instrumental, only L. uses of the exaltation of Jesus: cf. L. xxiv. 49, also i. 78 ἐξ ὕψους, of the place of God's dwelling for God Himself.

ἐπαγγελίαν, the thing promised, which consists of τ. π. τ. ἁ. gen. of apposition, for the continuing of the work of the incarnate life on earth (i. 8).

88. ii. 38 καὶ λήμψεσθε τὴν δωρεὰν τοῦ ἁγίου πνεύματος.

τοῦ ἁγ. π. again gen. of apposition or epexegesis.

δωρεάν, of πνεῦμα ἅγιον, v. 32, viii. 20, x. 45, xv. 8.

λαμβάνειν with τ. π., or similar phrase, viii. 15, 17, 19, x. 47, xix. 6, cf. i. 8, ii. 33; repentance and the baptismal rite being normally prerequisite.

89. iv. 8 τότε Πέτρος πλησθεὶς πνεύματος ἁγίου....

Cf. ii. 4, note; power given being manifested in 'speaking,' in his 'apologia'; cf. L. xii. 12. The 'filling' is special rather than permanent, 31, vii. 55, xiii. 9, etc.

90. iv. 25 ὁ τοῦ πατρὸς ἡμῶν διὰ πνεύματος ἁγίου στόματος Δαυεὶδ παιδός σου εἰπών.

The text seems to have been early corrupted here. D adds διά (after ἁγίου) and λαλήσας (before Δ.): a conflation may be suspected.

However, the usage διὰ π. ἁ. is in accord with the N.T. as regards the writers and speakers in Jewish history, cf. i. 2 of Jesus ; π. ἁ. being distinguished from God, as also 2 P. i. 21.

91. iv. 31 καὶ ἐπλήσθησαν ἅπαντες τοῦ ἁγίου πνεύματος.

ἐπλήσθησαν. Cf. ii. 4.

τ. ἁγ. π. Cf. i. 8 note.

A stately close taking up the language of L.'s summary of the Church's prayer, the common worship being accompanied or followed by external (ἐσαλεύθη ὁ τόπος) and ecstatic manifestations.

92. v. 3 διὰ τί ἐπλήρωσεν ὁ Σατανᾶς τὴν καρδίαν σου ψεύσασθαί σε τὸ πνεῦμα τὸ ἅγιον.... ;

Σ. Again in xxvi. 18 ; most frequent in L. (8 times), and 4 times in Mk ; keeping, as we should expect, the local colour.

Here τ. π. τ. ἁ. is certainly conceived personally ; lying to the Apostle (acc.) is lying to God's Spirit manifested in and through him, and so to God (4). Cf. i. 16 for full form ; cf. v. 32, 9, for same meaning.

93. v. 9 τί ὅτι συνεφωνήθη ὑμῖν πειράσαι τὸ πνεῦμα Κυρίου ;

τ. π. Κ. here only in Ac. ; besides π. Κ. viii. 39, also L. iv. 18 (in quotation). The O.T. flavour is preserved from the Aramaic sources of the infant Church : yet the style is markedly Lucan, e.g. συμφωνεῖν w. dat. only L. v. 36, Ac. xv. 15, and M. xx. 13 (of money agreement).

πειράζειν of God, also xv. 10.

[**94.** v. 16 φέροντες ἀσθενεῖς καὶ ὀχλουμένους ὑπὸ πνευμάτων ἀκαθάρτων.]

ὀχλ. at once reminds us of L. vi. 18 ἐνοχλούμενοι, both unique in N.T. ἀσθενής, 'invalid,' sick, so only the physician L., x. 9 ; Ac. v. 15, 16, iv. 9 (cf. 1 Cor. xi. 30).

πνεύματα ἀκάθαρτα in Ac. viii. 7 as well, but cf. L. iv. 33, etc. ; for πν. πονηρά, cf. xix. 12 and L. viii. 2 note.

95. v. 32 καὶ τὸ πνεῦμα τὸ ἅγιον ὃ ἔδωκεν ὁ θεὸς τοῖς πειθαρχοῦσιν αὐτῷ.

τ. π. τ. ἅ. sc. μάρτυς, elliptic; as an afterthought, 'the effect, too, of God's gift so manifestly displayed is also a witness.' τὸ...τὸ...well known as operative in them from Pentecost on. Cf. v. 3, ii. 33, i. 16. For refs. as to the 'gift' of the Spirit, cf. ii. 38 note. For the idea, cf. xv. 28 ; L. xxiv. 49.

πειθαρχεῖν, v. 29, xxvii. 21 ('we'), else only Tit. iii. 1.

96. vi. 3 ἄνδρας ἐξ ὑμῶν μαρτυρουμένους ἑπτὰ πλήρεις πνεύματος καὶ σοφίας.

πλήρης, metaph. only L., exc. J.'s 'prologue' (i. 14).

πλ. πνεύματος, or sim. v. 5, vii. 55, xi. 24 ; cf. also ii. 4 note.

π. κ. σοφίας, as we might speak of 'spiritual power and business capacity' in this connexion. For the combination, cf. Ps. Sol. xvii. 42, xviii. 8, of Messiah : also the interchange of the operations of Wisdom and Holy Spirit in the ' Wisdom ' literature ; cf. L. xi. 49. It is possible here, not preferable, to regard π. κ. σ. as a hendiadys.

μαρτυρουμένους, as also x. 22, (xvi. 2), xxii. 12, only Lucan in this sense. In passages such as these, whether the σοφία be regarded as supernatural or abnormal, we should see therein the development of innate rather than entirely new capacity ; cf. 5, 10 of Stephen's administrative and apologetic power.

97. vi. 5 Στέφανον, ἄνδρα πλήρη πίστεως καὶ πνεύματος ἁγίου.

πλ. κ.τ.λ. Cf. vi. 3 note, 10, and 8 χάριτος καὶ δυνάμεως.

πν. ἁγ. : L.'s favourite expression (Ac. 18 times). Cf. ii. 4 note, etc. To Stephen esp. it is ascribed, as his activity most promoted the Church's growth.

98. vi. 10 καὶ οὐκ ἴσχυον ἀντιστῆναι τῇ σοφίᾳ καὶ τῷ πνεύματι ᾧ ἐλάλει.

Again σοφία and πνεῦμα connected, cf. v. 3, but here σ. of

3—2

speech rather than organizing power. It seems hardly fanciful to acknowledge on L.'s part an artistic cross-reference to the Gosp.: xxi. 15 (σοφίαν ᾗ οὐ δυνήσονται...ἀντιστῆναι).

ἴσχυον, with this meaning, predominantly Lucan; L. vi. 48, viii. 43, xiii. 24, xiv. 6, 29, 30, xvi. 3, xx. 26; Ac. xv. 10, xxv. 7, xxvii. 16 ('we'), besides here: similarly also in Mk thrice, M. twice, J. once.

ἀντιστῆναι. Cf. L. xxi. 15; Ac. xiii. 8 (mid.). M. once.

99. vii. 51 ὑμεῖς ἀεὶ τῷ πνεγματι τῷ ἁγίῳ ἀντιπίπτετε.

Apparently 'memoriter' from Is. lxiii. 10 LXX.? παρώξυναν τὸ π. τ. ἅ. αὐτοῦ (H. וְעָצְּבוּ).

ἀντιπίπτειν, here only in N.T.; cf. Nu. xxvii. 14, late, LXX. רוּחַ קָדְשׁוֹ ultimately = יהוה as His operation personified; here and Ps. l. 13 only in LXX. trans. τ. π. τ. ἅ. The Apostolic spokesmen are ranked with the Hebrew prophets.

100. vii. 55 ὑπάρχων δὲ πλήρης πνεύματος ἁγίου ἀτενίσας εἰς....

Cf. for πλ. π. ἁ. vi. 3 note.

Presumably the utterance was in Aramaic, but the gist of it is expressed in distinctly Lucan style, whether his informant were Paul or Φίλιππος ὁ εὐαγγελιστής (xxi. 8), or some other ear-witness; so is also this introduction, e.g. ὑπάρχων, the vb is absent from Mk, M., J., while L.'s work has it over 30 times: ἀτενίσας, only L. and 2 Cor.; with εἰς, as here, 6 times (as the 2 Cor. two examples), but w. dat. twice in Gospel, in Ac. 4 times.

101. vii. 59 λέγοντα Κύριε Ἰησοῦ, δέξαι τὸ πνεῦμά μου.

Κ. Ἰ. some 12 times in Ac., freq. after ὄνομα. Even δέχεσθαι is predominantly Lucan: 14 times in Gosp., 9 in Ac., while Mk has 3, M. 6, and J. 1 example of it.

τὸ πνεῦμα, as L. xxiii. 46 ‖, viii. 55.

[**102.** viii. 7 πολλοὶ γὰρ τῶν ἐχόντων πνεύματα ἀκά-θαρτα βοῶντα....]

π. ἀκ.   Cf. v. 16, with ἔχειν L. iv. 33, Mk vii. 25.

πολλοὶ γάρ, πολλοὶ δέ, though the real subject of ἐξήρχοντο is πνεύματα : again there is a pathological contrast made between suffering from 'demonic' or other diseases.

βοᾶν, exc. in quotation, only L.'s writings (? medical).

103.   viii. 15 οἵτινες καταβάντες προσηύξαντο περὶ αὐτῶν ὅπως λάβωσιν πνεῦμα ἅγιον.

π. ἅ. λαμβάνειν, (i. 8, ii. 38 indirectly), viii. 17, 19, x. 47, xix. 6 ; cf. J. xx. 22.   Such an account seems almost certain to have come to L. orally, yet how Lucan is the dress !

οἵτινες, over 20 times in Ac.

προσεύχεσθαι περί...ὅπως, here only ; w. ἵνα, 2 Th. i. 11, iii. 1 ; Col. iv. 3.   ὅπως in M. twice, with 'entreaty' verbs, but L. 8 times (in Gosp. and Ac.).

104.   viii. 17 καὶ ἐλάμβανον πνεῦμα ἅγιον.

For phrase see above, viii. 15 ; the manifestations which betokened the power received continued (impf.) ; whether 'glossolaly' was always one of them (c. ii.) is never definitely stated.   Cf. J. xx. 22.

105.   viii. 18 ἰδὼν δὲ ὁ Σίμων ὅτι...δίδοται τὸ πνεῦμα....

ACD etc. and T. Rec. give the full form τ. π. τ. ἅ., perhaps through later Church influence.

τὸ πνεῦμα plainly takes up π. ἅ. of the former verses, and has the same meaning.   διδόναι, cf. ii. 38 n.

106.   viii. 19 ...ἵνα ᾧ ἐὰν ἐπιθῶ τὰς χεῖρας λαμβάνῃ πνεῦμα ἅγιον.

λαμβάνειν π. ἅ., viii. 15 n.

For the manifestations occurring in connexion with ἐπιτι-θέναι τὰς χεῖρας, vi. 6, viii. 17, ix. 17 (cf. 12), xix. 6.

107. viii. 29 εἶπεν δὲ τὸ πνεῦμα τῷ Φιλίππῳ.

In this portion, which we might call 'the Acts of Philip,' it is noteworthy how L. keeps the Palestinian colour of his stories; here the agent of direction is first described as ἄγγελος Κυρίου, v. 26 (like in O.T.), then as τὸ πνεῦμα, while the violence of the impulse (π. Κυρίου ἥρπασεν τ. Φ.) recalls the Elijah stories, and yet the general style is Lucan. The O.T. personification of inward voice and impulse seems to be true to the tradition.

For ἄγγ. Κυρίου, cf. v. 19, (vii. 30), xii. 7, 23, xxvii. 23 (θεοῦ), the first three (or two) in the 'Acts of Peter'; cf. too L. i., ii.; M. i., ii., xxviii. 2.

108. viii. 39 πνεῦμα Κυρίου ἥρπασεν τὸν Φίλιππον.

The supernormal impulse ascribed to π. Κυρίου is of the essence of the story, marking a step in the divine plan of the Christian Church's development (cf. i. 8, Jerusalem to Rome).

ἁρπάζειν, otherwise in Ac. only xxiii. 10 of the soldiers; cf. συναρπ. L. viii. 29.

πνεῦμα Κυρίου, here only (and L. iv. 18 qu.), but τ. π. Κ. v. 9; 2 Cor. iii. 17; as in 3 Regn. xviii. 12 etc. the quasi-personal (∥ ἄγγ. Κυρίου apparently) energy of God acting on special human instruments.

It is in accord with L.'s manner to attribute each 'crisis' in the Church's story to the Spirit. For the phrase, we may cf. En. xiv. 8, xxxix. 3; Ap. Bar. vi. 3, Bel 36.

109. ix. 17 ὅπως ἀναβλέψῃς καὶ πλησθῇς πνεύματος ἁγίου.

ἀναβλέπειν, of recovery of sight; cf., besides this and v. 18, Paul's account xxii. 13.

π. ἁ. πλησθῆναι, ii. 4 note; we may doubt whether, if Ananias used these actual words, the expression had the same permanent moral content as to Paul later on.

110. ix. 31 καὶ πορευομένη τῷ φόβῳ τοῦ κυρίου καὶ τῇ παρακλήσει τοῦ ἁγίου πνεύματος ἐπληθύνετο.

τὸ ἅγιον πνεῦμα, 8 times in L.'s work, only thrice else-where : cf. i. 8 note ; in each other occurrence in Ac. τ. ἅ. π. is that which, in fulfilment of the promise, should 'come upon' the disciples, and might be designated 'power' from God (i. 8), was given and received (ii. 38) ; and its 'filling' of individuals (iv. 31) in the Messianic community resulted in various re-cognisable manifestations of emotional or practical activities : in the sharing of such and impulse from such divine operation the παράκλησις consisted.

πορεύεσθαι, more frequent in L. than any other writer, but as here in a metaphorical sense (also L. i. 6 ; Ac. xiv. 16) peculiar to him among Gospel authors ; but cf. Ju. 11 ; 2 P. ii. 10 (ἐν w. dat.).

(ὁ) φόβος τοῦ κυρίου, the O.T. usage = יִרְאַת יְהוָה appears only in this instance in N.T., 2 Cor. v. 11 having a different complexion.

παράκλησις, xiii. 15 (by word), xv. 31 (by letter) ; cf. 2 Th. ii. 16 from God, so 2 Cor. i. 4 ff. (thus with the use of the word here the personal side appears), Heb. vi. 18 (indirectly through the promise) etc., while in the Birth-stories (L. ii. 25) π. virtually = Messiah, מְנַחֵם being one of his titles ; cf. παράκλητος of τὸ πνεῦμα τῆς ἀληθείας J. xiv. 16 etc., of Jesus 1 J. ii. 1.

πληθύνεσθαι. Cf. vi. 7, vii. 17, xii. 24 ; in Synn. only M. xxiv. 12 (eschatological).

111. x. 19 τοῦ δὲ Πέτρου διενθυμουμένου περὶ τοῦ ὁράματος εἶπεν τὸ πνεῦμα....

τὸ πνεῦμα, again of especial guidance for leaders in the Church, seemingly corresponding with ἄγγελος τοῦ θεοῦ in v. 3 as speaking to Cornelius ; cf. viii. 29 with 26.

For the opening gen. abs., cf. iv. 1, xix. 30, xxi. 17, xxv. 7.

διενθυμεῖσθαι, the compound only occurs here ; not class., LXX.

ὅραμα, only in Ac. (11 times) and M. xvii. 9 (of Transfiguration), but here, unlike *v.* 3, the ὅραμα and the inward
voice are distinct.

112. x. 38 ὡς ἔχρισεν αὐτὸν ὁ θεὸς πνεγματι ἁγίῳ
καὶ δυνάμει.

Isa. lxi. 1 seems to be in Peter's mind.

χρίειν, cf. iv. 27 in a Petrine address reflecting Ps. ii. 2
LXX., also L. iv. 18 from the same prophetic passage in
Jesus' synagogue address, and Heb. i. 9 qu. Ps. xliv. 8 LXX.
Otherwise, 2 Cor. i. 21 of baptism and τὸν ἀρραβῶνα τοῦ π.
with intentional play χριστόν...χρίσας: cf. the connexion in
1 J. ii. 20, 27. For the combination π. ἁ. κ. δ., cf. i. 8, with a
similar distinction, probably, of prophetic and wonder-working.

113. x. 44 ἐπέπεσε τὸ πνεῦμα τὸ ἅγιον ἐπὶ πάντας.

ἐπιπίπτειν hardly meets us in N.T. outside L.'s work: Mk
once, w. dat.; Paul once in quot. (Ro. xv. 3), and Apoc. xi.
11 in indirect quotation, both with ἐπί. So in LXX. of violent
emotion, especially fear, cf. Ex. xv. 16; Jud. xv. 2: of 'the
Spirit,' Ez. xi. 5: of τ. π. in N.T., Ac. viii. 16, xi. 15: of fear,
L. i. 12; Ac. xix. 17: mist, Ac. xiii. 11: figuratively of embrace,
L. xv. 20; Ac. xx. 37; cf. xx. 10 τ. π. τ. ἁ., as i. 16 n.

114. x. 45 ὅτι καὶ ἐπὶ τὰ ἔθνη ἡ δωρεὰ τοῦ πνεύματος τοῦ ἁγίου ἐκκέχυται.

v. l. τοῦ ἁγ. π. is strongly supported.   δωρεά, cf. ii. 38.
ἐκχέειν, of τὸ πνεῦμα, ii. 17, 18, 33.

The 'falling' and 'outpouring' were evidenced by acknowledged phenomena; cf. xix. 6.

115. x. 47 οἵτινες τὸ πνεῦμα τὸ ἅγιον ἔλαβον ὡς
καὶ ἡμεῖς.

οἵτινες, as L. so often for simple relative; cf. viii. 15 note.

τ. π. τ. ἁ. (or sim.) with λαμβάνειν, cf. ii. 38 note. In this
especial instance the manifestation preceded baptism 'in the
name of Jesus Christ.'

ὡς καί, cf. ὥσπερ καί, xi. 15 note, mostly Lucan.

116.   xi. 12 εἶπεν δὲ τὸ πνεῦμά μοι συνελθεῖν αὐτοῖς μηδὲν διακρίναντα.

L.'s favourite εἶπεν δέ once more, cf. viii. 29; about 60 examples in both portions of his work.   εἶπεν w. dat. and inf., cf. L. xii. 13, xix. 15.

συνέρχεσθαι, w. dat. L. only.

διακρίναντα, act., M. xvi. 3; Ac. xv. 9 and 1 Cor. (4 times) otherwise.   τ. π., as x. 19, viii. 29, xiii. 2, etc. at stages of the Church's progress.

117.   xi. 15 ἐπέπεσεν τὸ πνεῦμα τὸ ἅγιον ἐπ' αὐτοὺς ὥσπερ καὶ ἐφ' ἡμᾶς ἐν ἀρχῇ.

For the phrase, x. 44 note.

ὥσπερ καί, iii. 17, not else in N.T.; cf. ὡς καί, x. 47, xi. 17, xiii. 33, xvii. 28, xxii. 5; in M. thrice (vi. 12, xviii. 33, xx. 14).

ἐν ἀρχῇ, as also J. i. 1, 2; Phil. iv. 15: here of the Pentecostal phenomena (ii. 4; cf. xix. 6), of which 'glossolaly' was one.

118.   xi. 16 Ἰωάνης μὲν ἐβάπτισεν ὕδατι, ὑμεῖς δὲ βαπτισθήσεσθε ἐν πνεύματι ἁγίῳ.

Exactly as i. 5, words which Peter quotes in relating his experience : if spiritual baptism has been bestowed on a Gentile household, material cannot be refused; that is his 'apology.'

ἐν. π. ἁ., i. 5: cf. Mk i. 8 (without ἐν) = M. iii. 11 = L. iii. 16 ; cf. J. i. 33: this marked not Messiah only, but the new age.

119.   xi. 24 ὅτι ἦν ἀνὴρ ἀγαθὸς καὶ πλήρης πνεύματος ἁγίου καὶ πίστεως.

πλήρης π. ἁ., cf. vi. 3 note.

πλήρης...πίστεως, also in vi. 5 of Stephen, as here of Barnabas, only in reverse order.

πίστις, as opposed to ἡ πίστις of the Christian community,

is in these passages that keen confidence in the Risen Lord which is fruitful in missionary activity.

ἀνὴρ ἀγαθός, cf. L. xxiii. 50 of Joseph of Arimathæa. In Barnabas' case, as with the Seven, rather types of character seem marked, than ecstatic and occasional endowment.

120. xi. 28 ἀναστὰς δὲ εἷς ἐξ αὐτῶν ὀνόματι Ἄγαβος ἐσήμαινεν διὰ τοῦ πνεύματος....

διὰ τ. π., as of the friends of Paul at Tyre, in both cases of inward premonition.

Agabus belonged to the class of προφῆται (v. 27), however, and his reiterated assertions (impf.) as he stood in the assembly were through the instrumentality of his gift (διά) rather than ecstatic manifestation (ἐν π.).

One may suspect the originality of ὀνόματι Ἄγαβος, for in xxi. 10 he would hardly be formally introduced afresh by a writer of Luke's care in these matters. Here we have 'forecasting' for the Church's good.

121. xiii. 2 λειτουργούντων δὲ αὐτῶν τῷ κυρίῳ καὶ νηστευόντων εἶπεν τὸ πνεῦμα τὸ ἅγιον.

λειτουργεῖν, of Temple worship, cf. LXX. and Heb. x. 11; of men, Ro. xv. 27.

εἶπεν τ. π. τ. ἅ., cf. viii. 29 etc., like the Shekinah also. What a remarkably solemn and stately opening to the 'Acts of Paul,' the next stage in the 'Spirit'-guided evangelization from Jerusalem to Rome (cf. plan implied in i. 8); cf. westward guidance, xvi. 6.

νηστεύειν, in Ac. only in next verse (fasting, prayer, hand-imposition).

122. xiii. 4 αὐτοὶ μὲν οὖν ἐκπεμφθέντες ὑπὸ τοῦ ἁγίου πνεύματος κατῆλθον....

ὑπὸ τ. ἁ. π., also in xvi. 6 (κωλυθέντες), verses which easily lead over to a distinctively personified and personal view of τὸ ἅγ. πν. (agent more than agency); cf. the personification in O.T. apocrypha, and the distinct personality ascribed by the Rabbins to רוח הקדש; otherwise the occurrences in Ac. i. 8, ii. 38, iv. 31, (ix. 31) imply divine power given, filling, comforting, in its manifestation.

ἐκπέμπειν, here and xvii. 10; cf. ἐκβάλλειν, Mk i. 12. κατέρχεσθαι, only L. and Ja. iii. 15 : the former in correct (geographical) usage (G. 2, Ac. 11), the latter metaphorically.

123. xiii. 9 Σαῦλος δὲ, ὁ καὶ Παῦλος, πλησθεὶς πνεύματος ἁγίου....

The harmony with divine will of this fresh stage of Christian activity is marked by L.'s triple note of 'spiritual' agency in suggestion (2), in mission (4), and in effect (9).

πλησθεὶς π. ά., cf. ii. 4 note.

Σ., ὁ κ. Π. The Jew quits the stage of provincialism for the World-Empire, the national for the universal; but although we have passed to the freer style of the 'Gentile' chapters, as with Peter and John the 'filling' results in utterance, not in the wonder-working: cf. i. 8, ii. 4, iv. 10 ; also L. iv. 1 in contrast with e.g. xi. 20.

124. xiii. 52 οἵ τε μαθηταὶ ἐπληροῦντο χαρᾶς καὶ πνεύματος ἁγίου.

Another optimistic close; cf. ix. 31.   χαρά, also viii. 8, xii. 14, xv. 3. It is to be noted that μαθητής does not meet us outside Gospp. and Ac., not even in LXX., but in Ac. it passes from the Gosp. usage of 'the 12' and the immediate circle of followers into a designation for Christian community-members as a whole.   On the contrary, Mk, M., J., each have ἀπόστολος but once.   ἐπληροῦντο, cf. ii. 4, iv. 31, also of Church generally.

125. xv. 8 καὶ ὁ καρδιογνώστης θεὸς ἐμαρτύρησεν αὐτοῖς δοὺς τὸ πνεῦμα τὸ ἅγιον καθὼς καὶ ἡμῖν.

Peter, in view of his experience x. 44—47, pleads for the full community-rights of the Gentiles, as having received a similar manifestation to the Apostolic company at Pentecost; cf. ii. 4, viii. 18, xi. 15.

καρδιογνώστης, also in the prayer at the election of Matthias (i. 24); cf. בוחן לבבות Ps. vii. 10 Heb.

δοὺς τ. π. τ. ἅ. Cf. ii. 38.

καθὼς καί, only L. in Gospp.; cf. xi. 15 note.

126. xv. 28 ἔδοξεν γὰρ τῷ πνεύματι τῷ ἁγίῳ καὶ ἡμῖν....

This unique expression marks the conviction of the compiler concerning the fact of divine inspiration guiding the Apostolic leaders in the decision of the Conference, and emphasizes its importance in the story of the Church's development in the Empire. Cf. v. 32 of co-witness.

If it represent the original opening of the Apostolic encyclical, it is without parallel in early days, and Paul's letters but doubtfully imply any knowledge of a decree in this form, while the general style is thoroughly Lucan; even for this opening phrase, cf. ἔδοξεν in the Gospel preface, vv. 22, 25 in this context also, and τ. π. τ. ἅ. 17 times in Ac. alone. For the tendency later to add such words, cf. L. i. 3 where O. L. etc. insert 'et spiritui sancto,' and in this chapter (xv. 7) D and others add ἐν πνεύματι (before Πέτρος).

127. xvi. 6 κωλυθέντες ὑπὸ τοῦ ἁγίου πνεύματος λαλῆσαι τὸν λόγον ἐν τῇ 'Ασίᾳ.

Cf. xiii. 4 note, and v. 7.

λαλεῖν τὸν λόγον, tech. of preaching the Gospel; cf. xiv. 25, iv. 29–31, xi. 19, xiii. 46, xvi. 32 (Mk ii. 2, viii. 32).

128. xvi. 7 καὶ οὐκ εἴασεν αὐτοὺς τὸ πνεῦμα 'Ιησοῦ.

This unique expression, the originality of which is well testified by the MSS., seems to demand a unique experience, some vivid vision of Jesus; cf. in the Temple xxii. 18, yet in essence the effect is the same as v. 6. Cf. 2 Cor. iii. 17 f.

ἐᾶν only appears in L.'s writing and M. xxiv. 43.

[**129**. xvi. 16 παιδίσκην τινὰ ἔχουσαν πνεῦμα πύθωνα ὑπαντῆσαι ἡμῖν.]

π. π. Another expression unique in N.T. to designate the special type of 'possession'; cf. the demoniac witness checked by Christ, Mk i. 24 etc. The noun πύθωνα in apposition probably = μαντικόν ; cf. Plut. ἐγγαστρίμυθοι (LXX.) = πύθωνες.

ἡμῖν. We have entered the first 'we' passage, yet the manner is not changed.

παιδίσκη, L. xii. 45, xxii. 56; Ac. xii. 13 (Ac. of Pet., ? Mk); M. 1, Mk 2, J. 1.

ἔχειν, of πνεύματα etc., L. frequently.

ὑπαντᾶν, here only Ac., but L. viii. 27 (Gadarene), xiv. 31; also ·M. 1, Mk 1 (Gadarene ||), J. 4, and not else.

[**130**. xvi. 18 διαπονηθεὶς δὲ Παῦλος καὶ ἐπιστρέψας τῷ πνεύματι εἶπεν.]

τῷ π. as in the Gospels; the malign influence and the personality of the victim easily interchange as object of address or subject of action.

διαπονεῖσθαι, iv. 2 (of the effect on the Jewish religious leaders of the Apostolic preaching) also.

ἐπιστρέφειν, frequent in L.'s work; cf. xv. 36.

131. xvii. 16 παρωξύνετο τὸ πνεῦμα αὐτοῦ ἐν αὐτῷ θεωροῦντος.

The higher side of the 'self,' as the seat of feeling, emotion, trouble etc.; cf. xviii. 25, xix. 21; also Mk viii. 12 etc.

παρωξύνετο. Cf. 1 Co. xiii. 5, of love: παροξυσμός, Ac. xv. 39. τ. π. αὐτοῦ ἐν αὐτῷ, later pronominal redundance; cf. J.'s xi. 33, xiii. 21 of Jesus' deep feeling τῷ πνεύματι.

132. xviii. 25 καὶ ζέων τῷ πνεύματι ἐλάλει καὶ ἐδίδασκεν ἀκριβῶς....

Cf. above, on xvii. 16; for the expression, Ro. xii. 11.

λαλεῖν καὶ διδάσκειν, of 'preaching' and 'instruction' only here. ἀκριβῶς, outside L.'s writing, M. ii. 8 and Paul, 1 Th. v. 2; Eph. v. 15, besides.

133. xix. 2 εἰ πνεῦμα ἅγιον ἐλάβετε πιστεύσαντες;

For λαμβάνειν π. ἁ., cf. i. 8, ii. 38 etc.

The Messianic baptism ἐν πνεύματι ἁγίῳ the community of John Baptist's disciples had naturally not experienced.

πιστεύειν, abs. of believing the message of the Gospel, iv. 4 and often.

134. xix. 2 οἱ δὲ πρὸς αὐτόν 'Αλλ' οὐδ' εἰ πνεῦμα ἅγιον ἔστιν ἠκούσαμεν.

On the occasion of their avowal of faith, they had not heard of the special spiritual phenomena at Pentecost or accompanying Christian baptism. If John's message included π. ἅ., his disciples would hardly be ignorant of it; this verse seems to favour the absence of πνεύματι ἁγίῳ καί in M. iii. 11.

135. xix. 6 καὶ ἐπιθέντος αὐτοῖς τοῦ Παύλου χεῖρας ἦλθε τὸ πνεῦμα τὸ ἅγιον ἐπ' αὐτούς....

Taking up 2, on the imposition of the Apostle's hands the well-known manifestations occurred ; cf. viii. 17, x. 44 ff.

ἐπιτιθέναι (τὰς) χεῖρας, vi. 6, viii. 17, 19 n.

ἔρχεσθαι ἐπί, of π. ἅ., cf. i. 8 (ἐπέρχ.).

[**136.** xix. 12 τά τε πνεύματα τὰ πονηρὰ ἐκπορεύεσθαι....]

ἐκπορ., only in this case of evil spirits.

[**137.** xix. 13 ...ὀνομάζειν ἐπὶ τοὺς ἔχοντας τὰ πνεύματα τὰ πονηρὰ τὸ ὄνομα τοῦ κυρίου 'Ιησοῦ.]

For the 'name' in wonder-working, cf. Mk ix. 38 f.; Ac. iii. 6, iv. 10 : Jesus, too, admitted exorcism (M. xii. 27). For the importance of the divine Name (or names) in exorcism and curse magical formulae, we may recall 'Εφέσια γράμματα, 'Αβρασάξ, the various forms from יהוה etc., and the testimony of Inscrr. and Papyri.

[**138**. xix. 15 ...ἀποκριθὲν δὲ τὸ πνεῦμα τὸ πονηρὸν εἶπεν.]

The 'possessor' for the 'possessed,' cf. xvi. 18; M. v. 9 etc. Cf. L. vii. 21 note.

[**139**. xix. 16 καὶ ἐφαλόμενος ὁ ἄνθρωπος ἐπ' αὐτοὺς ἐν ᾧ ἦν τὸ πνεῦμα τὸ πονηρόν.]

ἐφαλόμενος, here only in N.T. (D has ἐναλλόμενος). Of πνεῦμα Κυρίου, 1 Regn. x. 6 etc.

τ. π. τὸ πονηρόν, in all these verses; elsewhere only L. vii. 21, viii. 2 (πνεύματα πονηρά), where a possible connexion in source of information was suggested. Compare Enoch xv. ⟨8⟩, 9, of the progeny of 'fallen' angels.

140. xix. 21 ἔθετο ὁ Παῦλος ἐν τῷ πνεύματι.

Here of the nobler aspect of human nature as sphere or seat of volition, cf. xx. 22.

ἔθετο, sc. βουλήν or sim.; cf. v. 4 ἔθου ἐν τῇ καρδίᾳ, of Ananias' secret arrangement.

141. xx. 22 καὶ νῦν ἰδοῦ δεδεμένος ἐγὼ τῷ πνεύματι πορεύομαι εἰς Ἰερουσαλήμ.

Cf. xvi. 6, xix. 21; Mk i. 12; L. iv. 1 of inwardly experienced compulsion, for in the human πνεῦμα the π. ἅ. of or from God has its sphere of activity; cf. xviii. 25: also M. v. 3, 1 Cor. vii. 34 for special qualities related to man's spirit.   δέειν, only here in N.T. of ethical obligation.

142. xx. 23 ...πλὴν ὅτι τὸ πνεῦμα τὸ ἅγιον κατὰ πόλιν διαμαρτύρεταί μοι....

But of such occasions we only have recorded xxi. 4, xxi. 11 as typical; cf. xi. 25 for foretelling among 'spiritual' phenomena. Utterances thus under the influence of π. ἅ. are ascribed to His agency, and so regarded as divine.

διαμαρτύρεσθαι, in 1 Th., Heb. once each, and Past. twice, besides L.

48 'SPIRIT' IN

143. xx. 28 ἐν ᾧ ὑμᾶς τὸ πνεῦμα τὸ ἅγιον ἔθετο ἐπισκόπους.

Again τὸ π. τ. ἅ. is represented as a personal agent, distinct from God, yet divine, witnessing (διαμαρτύρεται) yet also working in the Church in the appointment of its 'overseers' (ἔθετο). This personal activity is specially noted in a region which probably was the home of the Fourth Gospel: but the formula is Lucan; cf. xiii. 2, xv. 28 etc.

144. xxi. 4 οἵτινες τῷ Παύλῳ ἔλεγον διὰ τοῦ πνεύματος μὴ ἐπιβαίνειν....

Cf. xx. 23, foretelling, through the medium of the Spirit's (ecstatic) influence, as in xi. 28.

ἐπιβαίνειν, only Ac., but M. in quotation (xxi. 5). The Spirit is now means, now speaker (11).

145. xxi. 11 τάδε λέγει τὸ πνεῦμα τὸ ἅγιον....

We may liken the solemn formulae of O.T. prophecy, נאם יהוה, LXX. τάδε λέγει Κύριος etc., but apparently these utterances ἐν τῷ πνεύματι were not necessarily harmonious (xix. 21), xx. 22, xxi. 4, 11.

146. xxiii. 8 ...μὴ εἶναι ἀνάστασιν μήτε ἄγγελον μήτε πνεῦμα.

147. xxiii. 9 εἰ δὲ πνεῦμα ἐλάλησεν αὐτῷ ἢ ἄγγελος....

πνεῦμα, as a created being ἀσώματον, supra-mundane; cf. L. xxiv. 37 ?, πατὴρ τῶν πνευμάτων Heb. xii. 9; cf. Jub. i. 25 and En. often, also 'Lord of spirits': this seems more in keeping with Sadducaic rationalistic conservatism, than to refer it to the persisting part of human personality; sc. spirit after death, as freq. En. xxii., xcviii., ciii.; Ecclus. xxxviii. 23; Bar. ii. 17; Jub. xxiii. 31; 2 Macc. iii. 24?; 4 Ezr. vii. 78, for which some used ψυχή.

148. xxviii. 25 καλῶς τὸ πνεῦμα τὸ ἅγιον ἐλάλησεν διὰ Ἠσαΐου....

Of the Spirit of Jahweh speaking through the prophets,

cf. i. 16 note. It is Jahweh, not the Spirit, that 'speaks' to the older prophets, so that the later ascription of the Sacred Writings to the Spirit does not amount to identification, for just in this post-prophetic time angelological speculation was rife and God was not regarded as being in immediate contact with men.

In this Book, in accordance with Jewish views, the Spirit of and from God, however named, affects individuals in the Church of Christ in an occasional and special manner, and they are generally Apostles or men appointed by them; but also works within local churches gathered together as an aggregate in a more or less corporate capacity. Thus Acts approaches the fuller Pauline (and Johannine) doctrine of the divine Spirit's activity as inward, lasting, and catholic, among Christians as such.

§ 3. HEBREWS.

149. i. 7 ὁ ποιῶν τοὺς ἀγγέλους αὐτοῦ πνεύματα.

As LXX. Ps. ciii. 4 (A). The storm-wind and lightning-fire as other physical phenomena are personified as divine messengers; later Jewish speculation allotting angels to the winds, etc. (En. lxxii.–lxxix., lxxxii.). 'Wind' and 'fire' would remind the readers not only of the traditional details of the Lawgiving, but of the experience of the Day of Pentecost.

If the LXX. translation is patient of the interpretation 'spirits,' created spiritual agencies, the original undoubtedly demands 'winds.'

150. i. 14 οὐχὶ πάντες εἰσὶν λειτουργικὰ πνεύματα εἰς διακονίαν ἀποστελλόμενα;

The context compels us to leave the physical parallel. Angels, generically, are πνεύματα, and that λειτουργικά; 'spirits' will therefore be the only suitable translation here: that is their nature, cf. Ac. xxiii. 8, Jub. i. 25, διακονία the purpose of their mission : διακονία, only Paul and L., besides Ap. ii. 19.

So, too, fallen angels are πνεύματα, En. xv. passim. Cf. also the scenes in heaven, Apoc. xiv. 18, xvi. 5, etc.

λειτουργικός only here, but similar thought in Philo and Clement (1 Cor. xxxiv.), cf. also in idea Apoc. i. 4.

151. ii. 4 καὶ πνεύματος ἁγίου μερισμοῖς κατὰ τὴν αὐτοῦ θέλησιν.

Sc. συνεπιμαρτυροῦντος τοῦ θεοῦ (συνεπ. Clem. 1 Cor. xxiii.). μερισμός, only else in N.T. iv. 12, but of πνεῦμα ἅγιον cf. Pentecostal phenomena, Ac. ii. 3 διαμεριζόμεναι γλῶσσαι ὡσεὶ πυρός, 1 Cor. xii. 4 διαιρέσεις δὲ χαρισμάτων εἰσίν, τὸ δὲ αὐτὸ πνεῦμα, contrast J. iii. 34. πνεῦμα ἅγιον and δύναμις in close association Ac. x. 38, ii. 22 ; Ro. xv. 19, 2 Cor. xii. 12.

πνεῦμα ἅγιον, as often, the God-given operative influence behind the diverse manifestations, within the Christian, as successor of the Jewish Church.

152. iii. 7 διό, καθὼς λέγει τὸ πνεῦμα τὸ ἅγιον....

Quotation from Ps. xciv. 8 follows.

τὸ π. τὸ ἅγ. in this Epistle also ix. 8, x. 15; here and x. 15 an expression which seems but a circumlocution for God as author of Scripture, as this verse is reproduced in iv. 7 implicitly as God's words (cf. i. 1). This usage does not appear in Paul or Philo, but in Rabbinic writings, and there is no explicit identification : cf., too, Clem. 1 Cor. xiii., xvi., and Ac. xxviii. 25 reporting Paul's words. In later days more frequently the Shekinah is said to inspire the writers.

153. iv. 12 ...καὶ διικνούμενος ἄχρι μερισμοῦ ψυχῆς καὶ πνεύματος.

Boldly figurative to express the piercing and dividing power of ὁ λόγος τοῦ θεοῦ, affecting the whole being of man immaterial and material (ἁρμῶν τε καὶ μυελῶν). Human thought cannot separate the subject of life from the principle of life. It is unnecessary to assume a trichotomy, for it is no psychological definition, but a metaphor to shew how from the Logos 'no secrets are hid.'

διικνεῖσθαι not elsewhere in N.T., class., LXX.

ψυχή also vi. 19, x. 38, 39, xii. 3, xiii. 17, unlike Pauline usage: cf. distinction of ψυχή and πνεῦμα in 1 Cor. xv. 45 (mystical), 1 Th. v. 23 (popular).

154. vi. 4 ...καὶ μετόχους γενηθέντας πνεύματος ἁγίου.

πνεῦμα ἅγιον in He. only ii. 4 otherwise, where the reference is to the same divine power or gift, whose operation is experienced at the entrance of Christian life and growth; cf. the Pauline doctrine of Baptism, the effect should be permanent.

μέτοχος, i. 9 (qu.), iii. 1, iii. 14, xii. 8, and L. v. 7.

For the Spirit as ἡ δωρεὰ ἡ ἐπουράνιος, cf. Ac. ii. 38, x. 45, etc., 2 Cor. i. 22, v. 5, Eph. i. 14.

155. ix. 8 τοῦτο δηλοῦντος τοῦ πνεύματος τοῦ ἁγίου....

The priestly regulations (6 f.) are conceived to be God-ordained (cf. iii. 7, x. 15), to signify (δηλοῦντος) continually the inefficiency and imperfection of the worship.

δηλοῦν, also in 1 Cor. i. 11, iii. 13, Col. i. 8, 1 P. i. 11 2 P. i. 14, all rather of revelation, besides xii. 27. Class., LXX., Philo. Of this revealing the Holy Spirit is viewed as the agent, but there is no definite identification with ὁ θεός.

156. ix. 14 ὃς διὰ πνεύματος αἰωνίου ἑαυτὸν προσήνεγκεν ἄμωμον τῷ θεῷ.

v.l. ἁγίου, ℵcD*P, an easy alteration.

αἰώνιος, only here of πνεῦμα directly, cf. vii. 16 ζωὴ ἀκατάλυτος: that which ὁ χριστός has by nature as a heavenly

4—2

being enables His activity as priest to be carried on διὰ π. αἰωνίου or in the 'ideal' σκηνή or in αὐτὸς ὁ οὐρανός, and ἄμωμος too, as the law required for the earthly sacrifices, He is also victim (cf. 1 P. i. 19): each of these phrases for the 'spiritual' sphere has its opposite, its 'antitype' (χειροποίητα ἅγια, (ἡ) σκηνὴ ἡ πρώτη, δι' αἵματος) the within is contrasted with the without, the eternal with the temporal, and the efficacy transcends time, as does πνεῦμα (cf. J. iv. 24). Perhaps 1 J. v. 8 the 'idea' is conjoined with the temporal expression.

προσφέρειν, only Gospp. mostly M., Heb., and Ac. thrice.

157. x. 15 μαρτυρεῖ δὲ ἡμῖν καὶ τὸ πνεῦμα τὸ ἅγιον.

As ix. 8: here a quotation from Jer. xxxviii. (xxxi. Heb.) 33 follows, yet in i. 1 it is God Himself who speaks by the prophets, while what we should call the most mechanical view of the Spirit as source of inspiration is afforded in 2 P. i. 21 (ὑπὸ πνεύματος ἁγίου φερόμενοι).

μαρτυρεῖν, of Scripture testimony, vii. 17.

158. x. 29 καὶ τὸ πνεῦμα τῆς χάριτος ἐνυβρίσας.

For this descriptive gen. marking the special aspect of the activity of τὸ πνεῦμα, we may compare Zech. xii. 10 ἐκχεῶ π. χάριτος καὶ οἰκτιρμοῦ, also 2 Cor. iv. 13 (τῆς πίστεως), Eph. i. 13 (τῆς ἐπαγγελίας), and, if it be not rather of the resulting disposition, the anarthrous πνεῦμα δουλείας Ro. viii. 15, etc., while J. has the characteristic τῆς ἀληθείας xv. 26, xvi. 13, 1 J. iv. 6. This seems to accord best with the thought in ii. 3 f. and vi. 4 of the gift of divine grace bestowed after baptism.

ἐνυβρίζειν, here only, class., not LXX.

159. xii. 9 οὐ πολὺ μᾶλλον ὑποταγησόμεθα τῷ πατρὶ τῶν πνευμάτων καὶ ζήσομεν ;

Whatever be the range of τὰ πνεύματα, all spiritual existences, the primary application here is to our human spirits in contrast with (τοὺς) τῆς σαρκὸς ἡμῶν (πατέρας) in 9. For God as 'Lord of spirits,' cf. Nu. xvi. 22, xxvii. 16 and the title frequently in Enoch xxxvii. ff. (similitudes), Jub. x. 3, 2 Macc. iii. 24 ; Clem. 1 Cor. lxiv. (δεσπότης τῶν πνευμάτων καὶ κύριος πάσης σαρκός), lix. (τὸν παντὸς πνεύματος κτίστην καὶ ἐπίσκοπον).

ὑποτάσσεσθαι, cf. ii. 8, Ja. iv. 7, mostly in Paul and 1 P., L. thrice.

160. xii. 23 ἀλλὰ προσεληλύθατε...καὶ πνεύμασιν δικαίων τετελειωμένων.

πνεύματα of men as immaterial and persisting, cf. xii. 9. Although the cataclysm associated with the consummation is future (26 f.) the δίκαιοι, the men of faith (x. 38, xi. 4, 33, xii. 11), are conceived as already τετελειωμένοι through Christ in thought, whether of old or new dispensation (xi. 40, x. 14).

πνεύματα, cf. 1 P. iii. 19, iv. 6.

Cf. usage of ψυχαί in apocryphal books in similar sense of discarnate men (never angels), Jub. xxiii. 31, Wisd. iii. 1, En. ix. 3, 10, xxii. 9, 11, 12, 13 (Eth.), xxxvi. 4, cii. 5, 11, ciii. 7, and cf. Ap. Bar. xxx. 2, 4, li. 15 ; 4 Ezr. frequently ; Ps. Sol. ψυχή only ; cf. Apoc. vi. 9.

προσέρχεσθαι, a favourite word of this writer in the metaphorical sense of liturgic approach, cf. iv. 16, vii. 25, x. 1, 22, xi. 6, xii. 18, else only in 1 P. ii. 4.

§ 4. CATHOLIC EPISTLES.

S. James.

161. ii. 26 ὥσπερ τὸ σῶμα χωρὶς πνεύματος νεκρόν ἐστιν.

For σῶμα contrasted with πνεῦμα, cf. Paul often with an ethical colouring.

As in O.T. and apocryphal literature, πνεῦμα is here the unseen animating principle, cf. the divine πνοή of Gen. ii. 7, and in this case it is the thought of the 'breath of life,' cf. Apoc. xi. 11, xiii. 15, rather than of the higher nature that is prominent ; for the latter, indeed, we have found in some writings ψυχή and πνεῦμα interchange, often in parallel clauses, e.g. 3 Regn. xx. 4, 5, Isa. xxvi. 9, Ps. xli. 12; also ψυχή 2 Macc. vi. 30, vii. 37 ?, xiv. 38, xv. 30, Wisd. viii. 19, ix. 15, xv. 8, etc., and Ps. Sol. passim; of dead persons Wisd. iii. 1, 4 Ezr. vii., Enoch ix. 3, 10, xxxvi. 4, cii. 5, 11, ciii. 7, etc.; and πνεῦμα Jud. x. 13, 2 Macc. vii. 22, etc.

162. iv. 5 ἢ δοκεῖτε ὅτι κενῶς ἡ γραφὴ λέγει Πρὸς φθόνον ἐπιποθεῖ τὸ πνεῦμα ὃ κατῴκισεν ἐν ἡμῖν;

The doubt whether this is another rhetorical question or a direct or approximate quotation renders any certainty of interpretation very difficult.

It seems possible to take τὸ πνεῦμα either as the God-implanted nature whose responsiveness is the object of divine longing, supplying ὁ θεός from the context; or, as subject, the personified Spirit, the heavenly being indwelling us, more in accord with the Pauline idea (Ro. viii. 11 ff., Gal. iv. 6, etc.), but without special object expressed, sc. responsive human love. If κατῴκησεν, the v.l., be adopted, τὸ πνεῦμα must be subject.

κενῶς, only here in N.T.

ἡ γραφὴ λέγει, cf. Gal. iv. 30, Ro. iv. 3, x. 11, 1 Ti. v. 18.

φθόνος, Mk xv. 10=M. xxvii. 18, Paul 5 times, and 1 P. ii. 1.

ἐπιποθεῖν, seven times in Paul, and 1 P. ii. 2, but always with object expressed.

κατοικεῖν, in Ac. 20, Apoc. 15 times, Col. i. 19, ii. 9, Eph. iii. 17, Heb. xi. 9, 2 P. iii. 13, etc., mostly intransitive (cf. Ro. viii. 9, 1 Cor. iii. 16).

1 S. Peter.

163. i. 2 ἐκλεκτοῖς...κατὰ πρόγνωσιν θεοῦ πατρός, ἐν ἁγιασμῷ πνεύματος, εἰς ὑπακοὴν καὶ ῥαντισμὸν αἵματος Ἰησοῦ Χριστοῦ.

The phrase ἐν ἁγιασμῷ πνεύματος occurs 2 Th. ii. 13, but in a different sense; Ro. xv. 16 seems nearest the thought here, ἡγιασμένη ἐν πνεύματι ἁγίῳ.

For the coordinating of θεὸς πατήρ...πνεῦμα...'Ιησοῦς Χριστός, cf. 2 Cor. xiii. 13.

For the anarthrous expressions, cf. opening verses in N.T. such as Mk i. 1, M. i. 1, Apoc. i. 1.

Elsewhere in this Epistle τὸ πνεῦμα is bestowed (i. 11, 12, iv. 14), and is here regarded as the agent of the elect's sanctification, the gen. being subjective.

164. i. 11 ἐδήλου τὸ ἐν αὐτοῖς πνεῦμα Χριστοῦ....

ἐδήλου τὸ, so most moderns, B om. Χριστοῦ.

Accepting Χρ. as original, we are reminded of the view in Heb. of Christ speaking in Psalm and Prophet of old (Heb. ii. 11 f., x. 5 f., xi. 26) as here. It might be gen. of source, sc. sent by Christ, cf. Ac. ii. 33, but for O.T. times it seems better to take 'of Christ' as preexistent divine being. The principle of inspiration is the same in kind, cf. Heb. the speaker is also (interchangeably) τὸ π. or God, unlike in O.T. itself, where λέγειν etc. is not predicated of the Spirit. The process of salvation is one, but now viewed in the light of the Incarnation.

165. i. 12 ἃ νῦν ἀνηγγέλη ὑμῖν διὰ τῶν εὐαγγελισαμένων ὑμᾶς ἐν πνεύματι ἁγίῳ ἀποσταλέντι ἀπ' οὐρανοῦ.

Outside Gospp. and Ac. ἀποστέλλειν only meets us else Paul 4, Heb. 1, 1 J. 3, Apoc. 3 times.

ἀπ' οὐρανοῦ, sc. from God, primarily at Pentecost.

ἐν πνεύματι ἁγίῳ, of the influence under which the Evangelizers declared their glad-tidings, cf. L. xxiv. 49 ; it was God's, and yet Christ's (11 above). The repeated ὑμῖν...ὑμᾶς seems to mark the certainty and the privilege, and point the warning against apostasy.

εὐαγγελίζεσθαι, mid. else only in Luke and Paul : thus πνεῦμα (with δύναμις) is linked with τὸ εὐαγγέλιον 1 Th. i. 5, cf. with τὸ κήρυγμα 1 Cor. ii. 4.

ἀναγγέλλειν, mostly J. and Ac., cf. ἡ ἀγγελία, 1 J. i. 5.

166. iii. 4 ὁ κρυπτὸς τῆς καρδίας ἄνθρωπος ἐν τῷ ἀφθάρτῳ τοῦ ἡσυχίου καὶ πραέως πνεύματος.

πνεῦμα obviously here in the sense of disposition or character, cf. Gal. vi. 1 and probably Ro. viii. 15, etc.

ὁ κρυπτός, similar to Ro. vii. 22, 2 Cor. iv. 16, Eph. iii. 16 ὁ ἔσω ἄνθρωπος. The outward disposition manifests the inward and permanent as opposed to ὁ ἔξωθεν (3) and τὸ φθαρτόν, and such conduces to ὑποτάσσεσθαι (1). Cf. 1 Ti. ii. 8 ff.

ἡσύχιος, also 1 Ti. ii. 2, class.

πραΰς, M. v. 5, xi. 29, xxi. 5 else, class., LXX.

167. iii. 18 θανατωθεὶς μὲν σαρκὶ ζωοποιηθεὶς δὲ πνεύματι.

True ζωή is a matter of πνεῦμα the factor in human personality akin to God, and persistent beyond death, which ends the personal σάρξ-life, though Christ's π.-life preexisted (? i. 11). Paul's view is comparable, 1 Cor. xv. 22 ἐν τῷ χριστῷ πάντες ζωοποιηθήσονται, 36 οὐ ζωοποιεῖται ἐὰν μὴ ἀποθάνῃ (sc. seed), 45 ὁ ἔσχατος Ἀδὰμ εἰς πνεῦμα ζωοποιοῦν, with which cf. his use of ζωοποιεῖν, act., Ro. iv. 17, viii. 11, Gal. iii. 21 (of God), and J. v. 21 (God and Son), also J. vi. 63, 2 Cor. iii. 6 (of Spirit).

According to this passage, it is in His human πνεῦμα after death that Christ ministers in the abode of the dead (ἐν ᾧ, 19), unless Dr Harris's reconstruction (Expos. Nov. 1901) be accepted, continuing ἐν ᾧ καὶ Ἐνώχ...ἐκήρυξεν, in which case it was the translated patriarch who preached to the angels who sinned (En. xxi. 10).

168. iii. 19 ἐν ᾧ καὶ τοῖς ἐν φυλακῇ πνεύμασιν πορευθεὶς ἐκήρυξεν.

ἐν ᾧ, cf. i. 6, ii. 12, iv. 4, if πνεύματι not antecedent.

It is difficult to find any generally acceptable solution for this passage, if πνεύματα refers to discarnate dead (cf. Ap. Bar. xxiii. 4, 4 Ezr. vii. 95, contrast Heb. xii. 23) only as πνεῦμα could Christ preach to such, cf. i. 11 of preincarnate

influence ; but if Enoch be originally the expressed subject of
ἐκήρυξεν, the πνεύματα would be the star-spirits, the sinful
angels, such were bound in prison for ever, Enoch xxi. 10,
x. 4 f., 12 f., cf. also Is. xxiv. 22, Apoc. xx. 7 (Satan), 10
(torture of Beast and False Prophet), 2 P. ii. 4, Jude 6,
Enoch xxii. 3, Jub. v. 6, Tob. viii. 3.

πορευθείς, assuredly the preaching is immediately after the
victory over death and sin at the close of the incarnate life, if
predicated of Christ, and the recipients thereof need not be
limited to the Noachic generation (20) : perhaps Paul shews
knowledge of a victorious 'descent,' Ph. ii. 10 πᾶν γόνυ κάμψῃ
...καὶ καταχθονίων, cf. En. xlviii. 5 : but if πορευθεὶς ἐκήρυξεν
refers to Enoch, we find he is so told to proclaim to the sinful
watchers, Enoch xii. 4, and executes his mission xiii. 1 ff.
For the Messianic preaching, cf. Ign. Magn. ix. 2, Gosp.
Pet. 41, Herm. Sim. ix. xvi. 5, and for the joy thereat,
Enoch lxix. 26 : also Justin, Trypho, lxxi. f.

These verses must be taken in connexion with iv. 6, and,
if Christ be the preacher, the hearers there must include these
πνεύματα.

169. iv. 6 ἵνα κριθῶσι μὲν κατὰ ἀνθρώπους σαρκὶ
ζῶσι δὲ κατὰ θεὸν πνεύματι.

As in iii. 18 the σάρξ-life and πνεῦμα-life in contrast ; dats.
of reference ; there is also an implicit contrast of πνεύματι here
with καὶ νεκροῖς εὐηγγελίσθη.

No wholly satisfactory explanation seems available, but an
original comparison and contrast of Enoch and Christ may
well be now obscured, ζωοποιηθείς 18, πορευθείς 19 balanced by
δι' ἀναστάσεως 'Ι. Χ. 21, πορευθείς 22.

It is not clear who are the subject of κριθῶσι ; whether
iii. 19 refers to the rebellious spirits, or the disobedient before
the flood, this evangelization must relate to the nearer νεκρούς
in 5, with an allusion to Christ's sufferings σαρκί (1).   One
judgement seems general and future (5), the other special and
past (6), preparatory to continual life (ζῶσι) : may the en-

couragement for the present be derived from the example of suffering saints of old time? The difficulty of interpretation arises from our want of accurate knowledge of primitive Christian views on this mysterious subject of the descent: after all, the aim of the context is practical, the emphasis is laid on the ζωὴ κατὰ θεόν, and its blessedness, despite persecution, and the physical judgement of death.

170. iv. 14 μακάριοι, ὅτι τὸ τῆς δόξης καὶ τὸ τοῦ θεοῦ πνεῦμα ἐφ' ὑμᾶς ἀναπαύεται.

Apparently reminiscent of Is. xi. 2. The Spirit upon them (ἐπί acc. yet verb of rest) is characterized by δόξα in its end and by θεός in its origin, while the consolation of the presence thereof is coincident with the ὀνειδίζεσθαι of legal process, cf. Mk xiii. 11=M. x. 19, L. xii. 12. In i. 11 πνεῦμα Χριστοῦ is in near connexion with τὰς . . δόξας, and the δόξα idea recurs in 16, similarly marking the new dispensation 2 Cor. iii. 8, a foregleam of salvation. With such passages the thought of the Shekinah may be connected, as it corresponds closely in later Jewish teaching with רוח הקדש, and 'rests' on an assembly, Pirke Aboth iii. 2 b, 9. Cf. M. xviii. 20 promise of Christ's presence. It would be possible, though not necessary, to take τῆς δόξης as = Χριστοῦ here, in view of Ja. ii. 1, where τῆς δόξης is apparently in apposition to Χριστοῦ.

ἀναπαύεσθαι, only here in this sense; the divine Spirit, operative through the Messianic ruler of the old prophecy, is now regarded as operative on and in and through the Messianic congregation : cf. the record of Peter himself, Ac. v. 3 f.

2 S. Peter.

171. i. 21 ἀλλὰ ὑπὸ πνεύματος ἁγίου φερόμενοι ἐλάλησαν ἀπὸ θεοῦ ἄνθρωποι.

For ἀπό אAKL, etc., and Rec. Txt have ἅγιοι.

A metaphor, cf. Ez. iii. 12 etc., somewhat strong in expression, if the text be correct. πνεῦμα seems conceived as the breath of God personified; cf. for φερόμενοι, the driving of a ship by the wind (Ac. xxvii. 15, 17), Ju. 12. This writer abounds in anarthrous forms. For the apparently mechanical view of the mode of prophetic writing, cf. 2 Ti. iii. 16, Ac. iv. 25, etc., our minds go back to the old Hebrew and widespread primitive conceptions of the seer being inhabited by the god, and next, inbreathed by him; cf. even Philo's θεοφόρητος, Quis rer. div. her. 52, and his description of his own experience (de Migr. Abr. 7). Seeing that by the later Jews the Shekinah was regarded as a source of inspiration (Talmud and Midrash), a practical identification is suggested here, for in v. 17 above φωνή is attributed to the δόξα, the frequent equivalent of שְׁכִינָה.

S. Jude.

172, 173. 19, 20 οὗτοί εἰσιν οἱ ἀποδιορίζοντες, ψυχικοί, πνεῦμα μὴ ἔχοντες. ὑμεῖς δέ,...ἐν πνεύματι ἁγίῳ προσευχόμενοι.

A contrast is evidently to be drawn, and πνεῦμα must have a similar meaning in each case; here as so often, person and influence shade into one another, the divinely bestowed Spirit acting within is the motive power of action—corporate or individual, and the test here is an ethical one.

It does not clearly appear whether the act of ἀποδιορίζειν is regarded as evidence of the forfeiture of the divine πνεῦμα, Ja. iii. 14 f. connects such conduct with σοφία that is ψυχική, while 1 Cor. ii. 14 the ψυχικός is the one who οὐ δέχεται τὰ τοῦ πνεύματος τοῦ θεοῦ. ἀποδιορίζειν only occurs here in N.T.; it is difficult to assign the correct meaning, making separation or division, or, as between πνευματικοί and ψυχικοί in the Oriental and Gnostic manner making distinctions, and naturally boasting themselves to be the πνευματικοί.

ἐν. πν. ἁγ. προσευχόμενοι: prayer, spiritual in origin and ethical in result (21 ff.), cf. Eph. vi. 18 ἐν π. only, also 1 Cor.

xii. 3 of occasional and more violent manifestation, perhaps 1 Cor. xiv. 14 f. where human and divine are hardly separable. ψυχικός, soulish, natural, the principle of human and animal life dominant, instead of that akin to God through which the π. ἅ. works. The coordination ἐν π. ἁ…ἐν ἀγάπῃ θεοῦ…τὸ ἔλεος τοῦ κυρίου ἡμ. 'I. X. may be noticed (20 f.).

§ 5. PAULINE EPISTLES.

Romans.

174. i. 4 τοῦ ὁρισθέντος υἱοῦ θεοῦ ἐν δυνάμει κατὰ πνεῦμα ἁγιωσύνης ἐξ ἀναστάσεως νεκρῶν….

κατὰ σάρκα (3)…κατὰ π. ἁ. The contrast of σάρξ and πνεῦμα renders it necessary for us to regard π. here as a constituent part of the personality of Jesus, the higher aspect of His nature as man, only, as the unique medium of divine revelation marked by the attribute of holiness, cf. Test. Levi xviii., Heb. iv. 15 χωρὶς ἁμαρτίας. This includes, however, the wider interpretation of κατὰ πνεῦμα as 'on the spiritual side,' in regard of the inward, the eternal, this being further defined or characterized by ἁγιωσύνη. We meet this word again in N.T. only 2 Cor. vii. 1; 1 Th. iii. 13; LXX. Ps. xcv. 6, cxliv. 5; 2 Macc. iii. 12 (of the Temple); Test. Levi xviii. (above) of the saints eating the tree of life, having π. ἅγ. upon them : but for a scholiast, it is unknown outside Jewish and Christian literature.

For ἐν δυνάμει, cf. 2 Cor. xiii. 4 ; Eph. i. 19.

ὁρίζειν, class., LXX., in N.T. only Luke (xxii. 22; Ac. ii. 23, x. 42, xi. 29, xvii. 26, 31), and Heb. iv. 7 besides.

175. i. 9 ᾧ λατρεύω ἐν τῷ πνεύματί μου ἐν τῷ εὐαγγελίῳ τοῦ υἱοῦ αὐτοῦ.

ἐν τ. π. μ. In the sphere of spirit his λατρεύειν finds its activity, which is defined by τὸ εὐαγγ., i.e. the proclamation thereof; cf. xv. 16 ἱερουργοῦντα τὸ εὐαγγ. τοῦ θεοῦ. We cannot sharply separate sphere from instrument here; cf. 2 Tim. i. 3, L. i. 74, where the ἐν phrases could be adverbially rendered.

176. ii. 29 καὶ περιτομὴ καρδίας ἐν πνεύματι οὐ γράμματι.

ἐν π. οὐ γρ. forms a further definition of καρδίας; cf. σκληροκαρδία of LXX. (עָרְלַת לְבָב), the circumcision is spiritual as opposed to physical: for the contrast of π. and γράμμα, cf. Ro. vii. 6; 2 Cor. iii. 6, 7 f.; and for the thought, Ac. vii. 51.

177. v. 5 ὅτι ἡ ἀγάπη τοῦ θεοῦ ἐκκέχυται ἐν ταῖς καρδίαις ἡμῶν διὰ πνεύματος ἁγίου τοῦ δοθέντος ἡμῖν.

For the 'giving' of π. ἅ., cf. Ac. ii. 38 etc.

ἐκκέχυται, cf. 'outpouring' of God's Spirit, Ac. ii. 33, x. 45; Tit. iii. 6. The π. ἅ. imparted enables the Christian to have the sense of God's love, to recognize and appreciate it: ethical and lasting, 1 Th. i. 6; Ro. xiv. 17 etc. Cf. J. vii. 38 f.

π. ἅ. anarthrous after διά.

π. ἅ. in Paul 15 times, in Ro. 6 instances.

178. vii. 6 ὥστε δουλεύειν [ἡμᾶς] ἐν καινότητι πνεύματος καὶ οὐ παλαιότητι γράμματος.

Cf. ii. 29 above, 2 Cor. iii. 6.

The newness, the state in which service takes place, consists in its being 'spiritual' (π. gen. of apposition) as opposed to a written code: Love replaces Obedience, the Christian spirit the Mosaic law.

καιν., also Ro. vi. 4 ἐν κ. ζωῆς; cf. Ign. Eph. xix. κ. ἀιδίου ζωῆς.

παλ. here only in N.T., class.

179. viii. 2 ὁ γὰρ νόμος τοῦ πνεύματος τῆς ζωῆς ἐν Χριστῷ Ἰησοῦ ἠλευθέρωσέν σε....

ὁ ν. τοῦ π. τ. ζωῆς...ὁ ν. τῆς ἁμαρτίας κ. τοῦ θανάτου, cf. also vii. 23 ὁ ν. τοῦ νοός μου...ὁ ν. τῆς ἁμαρτίας. Where sin bears sway, death results (cf. vii. 10, 11); where the Spirit bears sway over the man in mystic union with Christ, life results: indeed the Spirit is itself life-giving (τῆς ζωῆς, gen. of apposition).

For πνεῦμα linked with ζωή cf. *vv.* 6, 11, 13; Gal. v. 25, vi. 8; 1 Cor. xv. 45; 2 Cor. iii. 6 etc.

180. viii. 4 τοῖς μὴ κατὰ σάρκα περιπατοῦσιν ἀλλὰ κατὰ πνεῦμα.

Cf. i. 4 and refs. for the antithesis.

The higher and lower aspects of human nature are treated as distinct regulative principles of a man's actions, contrasted as the old and the new, the unregenerate and the regenerate, the animal and the divine.

μή as usual with ptc., although in a few cases in P. οὐ has survived.

κατὰ σάρκα...κατὰ πνεῦμα, as also i. 4 (of Christ), viii. 5 etc.

181, 182, 183. viii. 5, 6 οἱ γὰρ κατὰ σάρκα ὄντες τὰ τῆς σαρκὸς φρονοῦσιν, οἱ δὲ κατὰ πνεῦμα τὰ τοῦ πνεύματος. τὸ γὰρ φρόνημα τῆς σαρκὸς θάνατος, τὸ δὲ φρόνημα τοῦ πνεύματος ζωὴ καὶ εἰρήνη.

κατὰ πνεῦμα in antithesis, as *v.* 4, cf. τὰ τοῦ θεοῦ...τὰ τῶν ἀνθρώπων φρονεῖν, M. xvi. 23; Mk viii. 33. The life is but the reflexion of the guiding principle whether higher or lower, earthly or Godlike, the human inwrought by the divine Spirit.

φρονεῖν, class., LXX., in N.T. Paul 23 times, Ac. xxviii. 22, and the above ref.

φρόνημα, also *vv.* 7, 27, not elsewhere in N.T., class.

ζωὴ κ. εἰρήνη, cf. viii. 2; the life is inherent as well as resulting: contrast vii. 10 and the preceding words. εἰρήνη seems too emphatic to form part of a hendiadys, it marks rather the peace of soul in harmony with the divine will as opposed to the 'war' inseparable from the 'fleshly' life.

For εἰρήνη and πνεῦμα cf. xiv. 17 (π. ἅ., cf. xv. 13); Gal v. 22.

184, 185, 186. viii. 9 ὑμεῖς δὲ οὐκ ἐστὲ ἐν σαρκὶ ἀλλὰ ἐν πνεύματι, εἴπερ πνεῦμα θεοῦ οἰκεῖ ἐν ὑμῖν. εἰ δέ τις πνεῦμα Χριστοῦ οὐκ ἔχει, οὗτος οὐκ ἔστιν αὐτοῦ.

The sphere of fleshly influence contrasted with that of spiritual influence; cf. also, with different connotation, 1 Ti. iii. 16; 1 P. iii. 18 (iv. 6; Gal. iii. 3).

In π. θεοῦ, θεοῦ denotes source: cf. v. 14; 1 Cor. vii. 40, xii. 3; 2 Cor. iii. 3, while Χριστοῦ seems rather to define or characterize the πνεῦμα; cf. Gal. iv. 6. Such a passage, however, is typical of the difficulty of interpreting or even of expressing exactly the various shades of meaning of πνεῦμα, where there is a mystical union between divine and human, and this self-manifesting in daily conduct, cf. Gal. v. 16 ff.

οἰκεῖ ἐν, involving a permanent effect on the Christian believer's life; cf. 11 n.

187, 188, 189. viii. 10 εἰ δὲ Χριστὸς ἐν ὑμῖν, τὸ μὲν σῶμα νεκρὸν διὰ ἁμαρτίαν, τὸ δὲ πνεῦμα ζωὴ διὰ δικαιοσύνην. 11 εἰ δὲ τὸ πνεῦμα τοῦ ἐγείραντος τὸν Ἰησοῦν ἐκ νεκρῶν οἰκεῖ ἐν ὑμῖν, ὁ ἐγείρας ἐκ νεκρῶν Χριστὸν Ἰησοῦν ζωοποιήσει καὶ τὰ θνητὰ σώματα ὑμῶν διὰ τοῦ ἐνοικοῦντος αὐτοῦ πνεύματος ἐν ὑμῖν.

One inclines slightly to regard the Western v. l. τὸ ἐνοικοῦν αὐτοῦ πνεῦμα as preferable (BDEFG O. Syr., O. Lat., Or. Ir. Tert. etc.) because of the context (10 and 2), thus taking the indwelling πνεῦμα as the reason of ζωοποιεῖν rather than the instrument of it.

For σῶμα in opposition to πνεῦμα (10, 11), cf. 13; 1 Th. v. 23; 1 Cor. v. 3, vi. 16, vii. 34, xii. 13, etc.; Ja. ii. 26.

τὸ π. τοῦ ἐγείραντος τὸν Ἰ., cf. 1 Cor. vi. 14, 2 Cor. iv. 14.

The interchange of expressions for the efficient cause is to be noted: with the above we have Χριστός, πνεῦμα Χριστοῦ and π. θεοῦ.

οἰκεῖν, class., LXX., Ro. vii. 20 (sin), 18 (good), viii. 9,

11; 1 Cor. iii. 16 (Spirit), vii. 12, 13 (μετά gen.); 1 Ti. vi. 16 (God), etc.

ἐνοικεῖν, also vii. 17; 2 Cor. vi. 16 (quot.); Col. iii. 16; 2 Ti. i. 5 (metaph.), 14 (of the Spirit).

190, 191. viii. 13 εἰ δὲ πνεύματι τὰς πράξεις τοῦ σώματος θανατοῦτε ζήσεσθε. 14 ὅσοι γὰρ πνεύματι θεοῦ ἄγονται, οὗτοι υἱοὶ θεοῦ εἰσίν.

πνεύματι, here of wider meaning than the exact antithesis (vv. 4, 5) to κατὰ σάρκα, for the new creation, the regenerate life, seems involved; so here it is hard to draw a clear distinction between the human πνεῦμα as a regulative power and the divinely originated and divinely bestowed π. θεοῦ, for just in this consists the kinship and the confluence of divine and human.

πρᾶξις, sing. only M. xvi. 27 (quot.), L. xxiii. 51, both implying evil: plur. here and xii. 4 (of bodily parts), also Col. iii. 9.

The metaphor (ἄγονται) must not be pressed too far; cf. Gal. v. 16 ff.: the 'sons' cooperate willingly.

192, 193. viii. 15 οὐ γὰρ ἐλάβετε πνεῦμα δουλείας πάλιν εἰς φόβον, ἀλλὰ ἐλάβετε πνεῦμα υἱοθεσίας, ἐν ᾧ κράζομεν ᾿Αββά ὁ πατήρ.

πνεῦμα δουλείας, here π. apparently more in our modern sense of frame of mind, the gen. characterizing or defining the particular disposition, e.g. in this instance the craven demeanour which a state of slavery produces as opposed to the free bright temperament of an adopted son.

π. υἱοθεσίας, cf. Gal. iv. 5; Eph. i. 5: such sonship frames the very address of prayer, as Mk xiv. 36.

For various qualifications of πνεῦμα we might compare, with an evil implication, π. ἀσθενείας L. xiii. 11; Ro. xi. 8 (quot.) π. κατανύξεως; 1 J. iv. 6 τ. π. τῆς πλάνης (cf. Is. xix. 14, π. πλανήσεως); cf. π. τῆς ἀληθείας...π. τῆς πλάνης, Test. Jud. xx.: also on the other side, π. συνέσεως Ecclus. xxxix. 6, π. τῆς δικαιοσύνης Enoch lxii. 2, τῆς προφητείας Jub. xxxi. 12, π. σοφίας Wisd. vii. 7 etc.

194, 195. viii. 16 αὐτὸ τὸ πνεῦμα συνμαρτυρεῖ τῷ πνεύματι ἡμῶν.

God as conceived in operation through the regenerate human πνεῦμα is Himself πνεῦμα, cf. J. iv. 24. By a process of self-analysis, the Christian's sonship-consciousness, which is itself the effect of the divine Spirit's influence, is found to be in harmony with his own feeling at its best and highest; cf. πνευματικός 1 Cor. ii. 15 f.

συνμαρτυρεῖν, also ii. 15, ix. 1; cf. for the thought, 2 Cor. i. 12: the source of this consciousness, this activity, is really personal—an αὐτός.

196. viii. 23 οὐ μόνον δέ, ἀλλὰ καὶ αὐτοὶ τὴν ἀπαρχὴν τοῦ πνεύματος ἔχοντες.

Preferably gen. of apposition, for τὸ π. is the ἀπαρχή possessed at present, the earnest of the future: τὸ πνεῦμα in all its varied manifestation of newness of life, social and individual, internal and charismatic, ethical and abiding.

ἀπαρχή, cf. xi. 16, xvi. 5; 1 Cor. xv. 20, 23, xvi. 15; Ja. i. 18; Apoc. xiv. 4. Class., LXX.

Compare 2 Cor. i. 22, v. 5, δοὺς τὸν ἀρραβῶνα τ. π.

197, 198. viii. 26 ὡσαύτως δὲ καὶ τὸ πνεῦμα συναντιλαμβάνεται τῇ ἀσθενείᾳ ἡμῶν...ἀλλὰ αὐτὸ τὸ πνεῦμα ὑπερεντυγχάνει στεναγμοῖς ἀλαλήτοις.

Cf. 16 both for idea (συν-) and expression (αὐτὸ τὸ πνεῦμα). The divinely bestowed gift is the subject, although the language is that of personification; the Spirit of and from God is ideally separated from the Christian, but really affecting his religious life from within. Christ affords similar aid, 34.

συναντιλαμβάνεται, also L. x. 40, LXX. (Ex. xviii. 22; Ps. lxxxviii. 22).

ὑπερεντυγχάνει, 27, 34 and xi. 2 similar in sense, only ὑπέρ separated. So too with Rabbinical writers the Spirit is regarded as witnessing to Israel before God (Wajjikra R. 6, etc.).

199. viii. 27 ὁ δὲ ἐραυνῶν τὰς καρδίας οἶδεν τί τὸ φρόνημα τοῦ πνεύματος, ὅτι κατὰ θεὸν ἐντυγχάνει ὑπὲρ ἁγίων.

ὁ δὲ ἐραυνῶν, sc. the Father; cf. Jer. xi. 20, xvii. 10, perhaps in the Apostle's mind here, applied to the Glorified Christ, Apoc. ii. 23: the vb also in J. v. 39, vii. 52; 1 Cor. ii. 10; 1 P. i. 11.

φρόνημα, viii. 6 of σάρξ as against πνεῦμα.

κατὰ θεόν, cf. 2 Cor. vii. 9 ff.

The operation of the divine gift which regenerates is necessarily in harmony with the divine will, as it guides the petitioning of the baptized (ἁγίων), experienced as distinct (personally) from God and the believer.

200. ix. 1 συνμαρτυρούσης μοι τῆς συνειδήσεώς μου ἐν πνεύματι ἁγίῳ.

The concurrent working of the divine Spirit with the human spirit, the highest aspect of man's nature, is here described by the Apostle from his own experience, and just as the πνεῦμα was personified (viii. 16), so here the συνείδησις.

ἐν πνεύματι ἁγίῳ, almost of the 'atmosphere' which the Holy Spirit causes, by and in His operation the union of human and divine consists for the Christian. Paul is convinced that by the Spirit God dwells in him, and also Christ dwells in him; the effect is the same, God-given guidance and inward conscience and the spoken (or written) word are all in harmony.

συνμαρτυρεῖν, ii. 15, viii. 16 above.

συνείδησις, mostly Paul: five times in Heb., 1 P. thrice; relatively late, LXX.

201. xi. 8 καθάπερ γέγραπται ἔδωκεν ΑΥΤΟΙC ὁ θεὸC ΠΝΕῦΜΑ ΚΑΤΑΝΥΞΕωC.

Quoting Is. xxix. 10 (π. κατ.) and Dt xxix. 4 (ἔδωκεν ὁ θ.).

κατάνυξις, cf. also Ps. lix. 4 (οἶνον κατανύξεως), and for various definitions of state or temperament with πνεῦμα, cf. viii. 15 n.

202. xii. 11 τῷ πνεύματι ζέοντες....

ζέειν, cf. Ac. xviii. 25 note, not elsewhere in N.T., class.

τῷ πνεύματι takes its place in the series of datives of reference; it is in the sphere of π. Naturally the human spirit through which the divine influence works.

203. xiv. 17 ἀλλὰ δικαιοσύνη καὶ εἰρήνη καὶ χαρὰ ἐν πνεύματι ἁγίῳ.

π. ἁ. of the power bestowed, in operation within the Christian continually, making for social unity, 15.

ἐν π. ἁ., also 1 Cor. xii. 3; 1 Th. i. 5. Cf. xv. 13, 16. For the thought, cf. Gal. v. 22; 1 Th. i. 6 (χαρά).

The joy arises from the consciousness of the influence within of the divine Spirit, cf. ix. 1 n.

204. xv. 13 εἰς τὸ περισσεύειν ὑμᾶς ἐν τῇ ἐλπίδι ἐν δυνάμει πνεύματος ἁγίου.

Similar to xiv. 17 in meaning (and cf. χαρά, εἰρήνη).

π. ἁ. gen. of apposition, that in which the δύναμις consists.

For δύναμις, ethical, not wonder-working in effect, connected with πνεῦμα, cf. 1 Th. i. 5; Ro. xv. 19? The experience of π. ἁ. is the earnest of the future: cf. ἐλπίδα δικαιοσύνης Gal. v. 5.

205. xv. 16 ἡγιασμένη ἐν πνεύματι ἁγίῳ.

Compare xiv. 17, xv. 13, of grace in operation.

ἁγιάζεσθαι ἐν, cf. J. xvii. 17, 19; 1 Cor. i. 2, vii. 14; Heb. x. 29; Ju. 1.

Yet it is God who sanctifies, 1 Th. v. 23: only the work of a divine Person can make the offering fit.

206. xv. 19 ἐν δυνάμει πνεύματος [ἁγίου].

If ἁγίου be retained as original (A, C, D etc.), cf. xv. 13 exactly: yet the meaning is unaltered if πνεύματος stand without addition. δύναμις seems to have a different significance from that in ἐν δυν. σημείων, unless the allusion be to occasional manifestations, then π. would be gen. of source.

207. xv. 30 διὰ τοῦ κυρίου ἡμῶν Ἰησοῦ Χριστοῦ καὶ διὰ τῆς ἀγάπης τοῦ πνεύματος συναγωνίσασθαί μοι....

τοῦ πν. gen. of source. The common spiritual gift (ἀγάπη) impels common action (συν-), as does the bond of a common Master. Cf. Gal. v. 22.

συναγωνίσασθαι, here only in N.T., class. If love be ascribed to the (personal) Spirit, cf. Ja. iv. 5.

1 Corinthians.

208. ii. 4 οὐκ ἐν πιθοῖς σοφίας λόγοις ἀλλ᾽ ἐν ἀποδείξει πνεύματος καὶ δυνάμεως.

ἀπόδειξις (class., 3 Macc. iv. 20, etc.), demonstration, which consists in (and arises from) πνεῦμα καὶ δύναμις, as opposed to λόγοι σοφίας of philosophic argumentation. For the collocation π. καὶ δ., cf. 1 Th. i. 5; Ro. xv. 13, 19; also Ac. vi. 3, 10 (π. κ. σοφία). Here it is practically a hendiadys, for the δύναμις is an attribute of the operative πνεῦμα. We are reminded of L. xii. 12. This power to produce πίστις is God's (5).

209, 210. ii. 10 ἡμῖν γὰρ ἀπεκάλυψεν ὁ θεὸς διὰ τοῦ πνεύματος· τὸ γὰρ πνεῦμα πάντα ἐραυνᾷ....

ἀποκαλύπτειν, esp. Paul (Ro. 3, 1 Cor. 3, Gal. 2, Eph. 1, Phil. 1, 2 Th. 3), the 'revelation' taking place in conjunction with the gift of the Spirit at the baptism (aor.) of the believer. διά, cf. Ro. v. 5.

τὸ πνεῦμα, in both cases the divine Spirit bestowed and working in and through the human πνεῦμα, and personified, the special aspect of operation being ἀποκάλυψις manward, ἐραυνᾶν Godward (contrast Ro. viii. 27).

211, 212, 213, 214. ii. 11–12 τίς γὰρ οἶδεν ἀνθρώπων τὰ τοῦ ἀνθρώπου εἰ μὴ τὸ πνεῦμα τοῦ ἀνθρώπου τὸ ἐν αὐτῷ; οὕτως καὶ τὰ τοῦ θεοῦ οὐδεὶς ἔγκωκεν εἰ μὴ τὸ πνεῦμα τοῦ θεοῦ. ἡμεῖς δὲ οὐ τὸ πνεῦμα τοῦ κόσμου ἐλάβομεν ἀλλὰ τὸ πνεῦμα τὸ ἐκ τοῦ θεοῦ....

Under this strictly imperfect because human comparison, we may not look for a Pauline analysis of the divine Nature. For it is not τὸ π. τοῦ θεοῦ τὸ ἐν αὐτῷ. A divine psychology on the analogy of human seems out of the question.

At baptism (aor.) the believer did not receive the spirit characteristic of the κόσμος, but of and from (ἐκ) God (cf. Prov. xx. 27), and this bestowal enables him γινώσκειν τὰ τοῦ θεοῦ: we may keep both the Person and His influence in view. The Christian attains to the knowledge of divine things only by the power from God, while his self-knowledge is intuitive, though the πνεῦμα, like συνείδησις (Ro. ix. 1), is ideally separable. Revelation through the spirit is a revelation of God by the Spirit. Though the language may not be pressed as a definition, it is a justifiable inference that the Spirit is within God (τοῦ θεοῦ), but in operation upon and in man experienced as ἐκ τοῦ θεοῦ, and it is the manward aspect that is emphasized here.

215. ii. 13 ἃ γὰρ λαλοῦμεν οὐκ ἐν διδακτοῖς ἀνθρω-πίνης σοφίας λόγοις, ἀλλ' ἐν διδακτοῖς πνεύματος, πνευματικοῖς πνευματικὰ συνκρίνοντες.

The addition of ἁγίου by later copyists shows a tendency which has perhaps already affected our best texts. The πνεῦμα (cf. ii. 4) received is the instrument of instruction for the believer as the rhetorical training of the schools for the non-Christian speaker. Such seems the interpretation best suiting the Apostolic comment, 'linking spiritual things with spiritual things' (if with 13), 'men' (if with 14).

For the anarthrous balance of σοφία and π. cf. ii. 4.

For the Spirit teaching, cf. L. xii. 12, Bereshith R. 85.

216. ii. 14 ψυχικὸς δὲ ἄνθρωπος οὐ δέχεται τὰ τοῦ πνεύματος τοῦ θεοῦ.

ψυχικός almost = σαρκικός, opposed to πνευματικός, cf. xv.

44 ff. (*ter*) of σῶμα; Ja. iii. 15 of σοφία that is not ἄνωθεν; Jude 19, explained by πνεῦμα μὴ ἔχοντες. For the moral contrast cf. Ro. viii. 4 ff.

τ. π. τοῦ θεοῦ, cf. 11, 12 and explanation offered.

A slight suspicion is raised by the omission of τοῦ θεοῦ (in 2 and others), because the tendency was almost invariably to complete rather than omit. Ultimately the source is personal, but manifested through the human instrument (13).

217. iii. 16 οὐκ οἴδατε ὅτι ναὸς θεοῦ ἐστε καὶ τὸ πνεῦμα τοῦ θεοῦ ἐν ὑμῖν οἰκεῖ;

The presence of the Spirit in the community is regarded as in some sense the token of the divine Presence, cf. the Shekinah (Pirke Ab. iii. 2 b).

For οἰκεῖν of τὸ πνεῦμα, cf. Ro. viii. 9 ff. etc.

May not the Greek conception of the god inhabiting his sanctuary, and indwelling the initiated, be present to the Apostle? The address is general, but the indwelling, with Paul, primarily individual; it is putting into words the vivid realization of a personal indwelling presence.

218. iv. 21 ἐν ῥάβδῳ ἔλθω πρὸς ὑμᾶς, ἢ ἐν ἀγάπῃ πνεύματί τε πραΰτητος;

πραΰτητος, adjectival genitive, the meek or gentle frame of mind being an accompaniment of ἀγάπη, itself a fruit of the Spirit (Gal. v. 16).

πνεῦμα qualified by genitive, cf. Ro. xi. 8 etc.; 2 Cor. iv. 13; Eph. i. 17 (divine gift).

ἐν ῥάβδῳ, cf. Apoc. ii. 27, xii. 5, xix. 15.

219, 220, 221. v. 3 ἀπὼν τῷ σώματι παρὼν δὲ τῷ πνεύματι.... 4 συναχθέντων ὑμῶν καὶ τοῦ ἐμοῦ πνεύματος.... 5 ἵνα τὸ πνεῦμα σωθῇ ἐν τῇ ἡμέρᾳ τοῦ κυρίου.

For 3 f., compare ἡ καρδία of Elisha, 4 Regn. v. 26; also Col. ii. 5 τῇ σαρκὶ ἄπειμι, ἀλλὰ τῷ πνεύματι σὺν ὑμῖν εἰμί. Paul never contrasts σῶμα and ψυχή. In harmony of mind, in sympathy of thought, Paul's behests and expressed desires are to be treated as though he were personally and visibly present.

5. τὸ πνεῦμα, the persisting and (cf. Enoch) redeemable element of human personality, in contrast with the σάρξ, whose suffering, inflicted by Σατανᾶς, is regarded by Paul as remedial; cf. L. xxii. 31, 2 Cor. xii. 7, Heb. ii. 14 etc.

ἡ ἡμέρα (τοῦ κυρίου), cf. i. 8, iii. 13 (iv. 5), v. 5; 2 Cor. i. 14; Eph. iv. 30 (ἡμ. ἀπολυτρώσεως); Phil. i. 6 (ἡμ. Ἰ. Χ.), 10, ii. 16 (ἡμ. Χ.); 1 Th. v. 2 (ἡμ. Κ.), 4 (ἡ ἡμ.); 2 Th. i. 10 (ἡ ἡμ. ἐκείνη), ii. 2 (ἡ ἡμ. τ. κ.); while in the Pastorals we have ἐκείνη ἡ ἡμ. 2 Ti. i. 12, 18, iv. 8, and likewise in Ro. ἡμ. ὀργῆς ii. 5, ἡμ. ὅτε κρινεῖ ὁ θεός ii. 16, and absol. xiii. 12.

222. vi. 11 ἀλλὰ ἐδικαιώθητε ἐν τῷ ὀνόματι τοῦ κυρίου [ἡμῶν] Ἰησοῦ Χριστοῦ καὶ ἐν τῷ πνεύματι τοῦ θεοῦ ἡμῶν.

The primary allusion is apparently to the event of the believer's baptism when the action was in the Lord's name (cf. Ac.), and the bestowal of τὸ πνεῦμα was regarded as coincident in time (Ac. x. 47–8, xix. 5; cf. Tit. iii. 5 f.). The ancient views of the potency of 'the name' of God or demon form too wide a subject to touch here.

δικαιωθῆναι, the pf. also is used of the occasion of baptism in Ro. vi. 7.

τ. π. τοῦ θεοῦ, as ii. 11, 14, iii. 16; (Eph. iv. 30).

223. vi. 17 ὁ δὲ κολλώμενος τῷ κυρίῳ ἓν πνεῦμά ἐστιν.

In vivid and balanced contrast to the fleshly union (v. 16): for this mystic union of spirit, cf. spiritual 'body' of which individuals are members (v. 15), cf. Eph. iv. 4: it is self-identification rather than absorption, and that because ὁ κύριος is Himself πνεῦμα ζωοποιοῦν, xv. 45; and the union is lasting.

κολλᾶσθαι, 16; Ro. xii. 9; 7 times in L. and Ac.; M. xix. 5 qu.; Ap. xviii. 5. Cf. Dt. x. 20 metaph. of Israel.

224. vi. 19 ἢ οὐκ οἴδατε ὅτι τὸ σῶμα ὑμῶν ναὸς τοῦ ἐν ὑμῖν ἁγίου πνεύματός ἐστιν, οὗ ἔχετε ἀπὸ θεοῦ ;

Cf. iii. 16 τὸ ἅγιον πνεῦμα or τὸ πνεῦμα is treated as τοῦ θεοῦ there, ἐκ τοῦ θεοῦ ii. 12, ἀπὸ θεοῦ in this verse.

The Spirit-gift from God is conceived as enshrined in Christians collectively (iii. 16) and individually (here). Paul's language wavers between a Person living within him or His influence ; but the effect described is the same.

225. vii. 34 ἵνα ᾖ ἁγία [καὶ] τῷ σώματι καὶ τῷ πνεύματι.

σῶμα καὶ πνεῦμα to cover the entire personality, cf. also v. 3 ; Ro. viii. 10 etc.

Holiness, the aim of the single-minded, dedicated life, is an essential quality of God and of the Spirit that is of or from Him, and so, ideally, of the human being belonging to Him.

226. vii. 40 δοκῶ γὰρ κἀγὼ πνεῦμα θεοῦ ἔχειν.

δοκεῖν, cf. iii. 18, viii. 2, x. 12, xiv. 37 in this letter.

κἀγώ, in gentle irony, 'surely I too have the divine Spirit operating within me !'

π. θεοῦ, as Ro. viii. 9, 14 ; 2 Cor. iii. 3, both without, or else both with, article in Paul : see also xii. 3.

For ἔχειν, the inward possession, cf. vi. 19.

227, 228. xii. 3 οὐδεὶς ἐν πνεύματι θεοῦ λαλῶν λέγει· ΑΝΑΘΕΜΑ ΙΗΣΟΥΣ, καὶ οὐδεὶς δύναται εἰπεῖν· ΚΥΡΙΟΣ ΙΗΣΟΥΣ, εἰ μὴ ἐν πνεύματι ἁγίῳ.

Here ἐν π. θ. and ἐν π. ἁγίῳ are equivalent ; cf. refs. above with Ro. xiv. 17, xv. 13, 16. Unconscious ecstatic utterance was sometimes so uncontrolled, that appalling words were said ; an observed fact in times of 'revival'; though perhaps the Apostle tacitly implies 'demonic' influence.

The phenomena, exceptionally acute at Corinth, were in early days almost regarded as being normal with the baptized in assembly : and the regulative influence of Paul in these chapters is in the cause of order (cf. Acts, and the Montanist reaction). The Spirit is called by Paul now God's, now Christ's, so the working thereof can only be to the honour of Jesus in deed or, as here, word : a man's recognition of Jesus is the Spirit's work (cf. 1 J. iv. 2).

229. xii. 4 διαιρέσεις δὲ χαρισμάτων εἰσίν, τὸ δὲ αὐτὸ πνεῦμα.

The source is one, bestowed on all, though the manifestations of its operations are various. Though the expressions in these *vv.* name (each with ὁ αὐτὸς) πνεῦμα, κύριος, θεός, and naturally figured in the development of Trinitarian doctrine, they afford material for it, without any formal idea thereof being present to Paul's mind (cf. 2 Cor. xiii. 13, Eph. iv. 4 ff.). God is ὁ ἐνεργῶν (6), yet τ. π. ἐνεργεῖ (11).

διαιρέσεις, kinds resulting from (ideal) subdivision, cf. 5, 6 also (vb xii. 11 and Lk xv. 12, of distribution of goods). In LXX. cf. use of Temple ' courses ' of priests. The διαιρέσεις from another point of sight are φανερώσεις (7).

χαρίσματα, Ro. xi. 29, xii. 6 ; 1 Cor. xii. 9, 28, 30, 31 ; sing. Ro. i. 11, v. 15, 16, vi. 23 ; 1 Cor. i. 7, vii. 7 ; 2 Cor. i. 11 ; 1 Ti. iv. 14 ; 2 Ti. i. 6 ; outside Paul's writings, only 1 Pet. iv. 10 ; also in Philo, not LXX.

230, 231, 232, 233, 234. xii. 7 ἑκάστῳ δὲ δίδοται ἡ φανέρωσις τοῦ πνεύματος πρὸς τὸ συμφέρον. 8 ᾧ μὲν γὰρ διὰ τοῦ πνεύματος δίδοται λόγος σοφίας, ἄλλῳ δὲ λόγος γνώσεως κατὰ τὸ αὐτὸ πνεῦμα, 9 ἑτέρῳ πίστις ἐν τῷ αὐτῷ πνεύματι, 10 ἄλλῳ δὲ χαρίσματα ἰαμάτων ἐν τῷ ἑνὶ πνεύματι.

ἡ φαν. τ. πνεύματος, gen. rather subjective than of apposition, the same thought of one gift in various manifestation in different individuals runs through these verses.

λόγος has an unique shade of meaning here ; the faculty of speech and argument which usually comes by training, characterized by σοφία, γνῶσις, arises from τὸ πνεῦμα, cf. ii. 13, 6.

The variety of expression (διά, κατά, ἐν; αὐτό, ἕν) seems hardly to be attributed to minute technical distinction, but rather breaks a monotonous repetition, the following verses serving to exemplify and illustrate v. 7.

No doubt behind the linguistically neuter wording there lies the thought of the one Person, and that divine, whose influence comes out in a φανέρωσις in each several member, yet with such διαίρεσις of kind. (Cf. also Heb. ii. 4.)

235. xii. 10 ἄλλῳ [δὲ] διακρίσεις πνευμάτων.

πνεύματα, pl. the cause (or causes) named for the effects thereof, the utterances of various persons in the assembly, men ἐν πνεύματι θεοῦ λαλοῦντες or not: if it be regarded as meaning discriminating the sources of these manifestations rather than the results themselves: cf. 2 Th. ii. 2, 1 Ti. iv. 1, 1 J. iv. 1.

236. xii. 11 πάντα δὲ ταῦτα ἐνεργεῖ τὸ ἓν καὶ τὸ αὐτὸ πνεῦμα, διαιροῦν ἰδίᾳ ἑκάστῳ καθὼς βούλεται.

ἐνεργεῖ, only Mk, M., Ja. once each outside Paul.
διαιροῦν, cf. xii. 4 n.

With all the diversity of phenomena, ordinary or extra-ordinary, that mark its operation in individuals, this divine influence outpoured, given, or indwelling, is emphatically one and the same in origin, hence to a church full of faction and jealousy a great incentive to unity; and the activities are such as can be ascribed only to a personal divine source (ἐνεργεῖ) that wills (βούλεται), from Whom, ultimately, the manifestation in each and all emanates. Though unexpressed, the inference is that τὸ π. is θεός; cf. χii. 6 ὁ δὲ αὐτὸς θεὸς ὁ ἐνεργῶν τὰ πάντα ἐν πᾶσιν, and J. v. 21 θέλει of ὁ υἱός.

237, 238. xii. 13 καὶ γὰρ ἐν ἑνὶ πνεύματι ἡμεῖς πάντες εἰς ἓν σῶμα ἐβαπτίσθημεν...καὶ πάντες ἓν πνεῦμα ἐποτίσθημεν.

Again the close association of the πνεῦμα with baptism (cf. M. iii. 11 etc.), again the oneness of the gift as a plea for unity among the recipients, seeing that like a common cup they all partook of it (? analogy of Eucharistic cup).

A totally different metaphor is used 2 Cor. iii. 3.

ποτίζειν, only figurative in P. (here and iii. 2 ff.) except Ro. xii. 20 (qu.), class., LXX.; passive in this verse alone.

The recurring πάντες and ἕν take up πάντα...ἕν of previous verses, and the series forms a remarkable cumulative argument followed by the reasoning from physical analogy.

239. xiv. 2 πνεύματι δὲ λαλεῖ μυστήρια.

The glossolaly is not intelligible (οὐδεὶς γὰρ ἀκούει); πνεύματι naturally of the man who is the agent: only if one be present gifted with ἑρμηνεία γλωσσῶν (5, 27) can there be interpretation of the incoherent sounds, that are deeply emotional and involuntary.

πνεύματι, cf. 14; Ro. i. 9 etc., not generally anarthrous.

μυστήρια, outside Paul only M. xiii. 11; Mk iv. 11 (sing.); Apoc. i. 20, x. 7, xvii. 5, 7 (all sing.). Plur. here and iv. 1, xiii. 2, of secret things revealed; LXX. also.

240. xiv. 12 ἐπεὶ ζηλωταί ἐστε πνευμάτων.

Again (cf. xii. 10) the word designating the cause used for its manifestations or effects; 'inspirations' would be to us a less ambiguous rendering than 'spirits,' as also in 32.

ζηλωτής, only L. (of Simon, vi. 15; Ac. i. 13); Gal. i. 14; Tit. ii. 14; 1 P. iii. 13 else: class., LXX.

241. xiv. 14 τὸ πνεῦμά μου προσεύχεται, ὁ δὲ νοῦς μου ἄκαρπός ἐστιν.

The agent is conscious of ecstatic prayer, but has neither control of words nor knowledge of the purport of the utterance; the activity of the νοῦς is suspended. Paul can speak of this from his own experience, 18 πάντων ὑμῶν μᾶλλον γλώσσαις λαλῶ. πνεῦμα and νοῦς are contrasted only in this passage, 14 f., though νοῦς as the purely intellectual part of the higher nature of man occurs too 2 Th. ii. 2; Ro. vii. 25; mostly in

Paul's writings more general, of mind or state of mind, and (Ro. vii. 25) like πνεῦμα, opposed to σάρξ.

ἄκαρπος, lit. M. xiii. 22 and ‖ Mk iv. 19; Jude 12 (of Christians as δένδρα); fig. also Eph. v. 11, Tit. iii. 14, 2 Pet. i. 8 (Jude adapted).

242, 243. xiv. 15 προσεύξομαι τῷ πνεύματι, προσεύξομαι δὲ καὶ τῷ νοΐ· ψαλῶ τῷ πνεύματι, ψαλῶ δὲ καὶ τῷ νοΐ.

So prayer and singing that are conscious, and not only in uncontrolled ecstasy, are more profitable both to the individual and to the assembly: cf. 14; hence articles here.

244. xiv. 16 ἐπεὶ ἐὰν εὐλογῇς [ἐν] πνεύματι.

As in v. 2, πνεύματι meaning in the ecstatic condition induced by spirit influence, the special manifestation being 'glossolaly.' Under such circumstances eucharistic prayer would not be comprehended, and the ἀμήν would be meaningless.

If the distinctions are to be pressed, π. is sphere in this case, as instrument (15) and subject (14) before.

245. xiv. 32 καὶ πνεύματα προφητῶν προφήταις ὑποτάσσεται.

πνεύματα. Cf. v. 12, 'spirits' = spiritual manifestations, effects of the indwelling πνεῦμα, 'inspirations.' Reiterating in the cause of order (cf. 40) the plea for conscious worship in place of the jealous desire for startling and abnormal phenomena (cf. v. 15, of the control of the reason).

ὑποτάσσειν, esp. in Ro., 1 Cor., Eph. (Lk 3, Heb. 5, 1 Pet. 6). The προφῆται, speaking comprehensible words, are subject to the estimate and criticism of others under the same influence; the plural (πνεύματα) suggests this to be the meaning rather than the personal control over the prophet's own utterance.

246. xv. 45 ὁ ἔσχατος Ἀδὰμ εἰς πνεῦμα ζωοποιοῦν.

Thus the contrast and advance are marked: 'the first 'man' Adam after πνοή of God entered him became ψυχὴ ζῶσα, created; Christ, in risen glorified πνεῦμα-life, became rather 'life-giving,' creative, 22 f.

ζωοποιεῖν, in post-Pauline writings cf. J. v. 21 of ὁ πατήρ and ὁ υἱός, vi. 63 of τὸ πνεῦμα opposed to ἡ σάρξ; also 1 Pet. iii. 18 ζωοποιηθείς δὲ πνεύματι (of Christ Himself?); in Paul, Ro. iv. 17, viii. 11, of God 'quickening' the dead; 1 Cor. xv. 22, 36 (pass.) ἐν τῷ χριστῷ and of ὃ σπείρεις; 2 Cor. iii. 6 (τὸ πνεῦμα); Gal. iii. 21 (God).

247. xvi. 18 ἀνέπαυσαν γὰρ τὸ ἐμὸν πνεῦμα καὶ τὸ ὑμῶν.

A sympathetic touch of self-identification with the Corinthians, a part of the personality being put for his whole self.

For the thought, cf. Ro. xv. 32; 2 Cor. vii. 13; Phlm. 7, 20 (σπλάγχνα).

2 Corinthians.

248. i. 22 [ὁ] καὶ σφραγισάμενος ἡμᾶς καὶ δοὺς τὸν ἀρραβῶνα τοῦ πνεύματος ἐν ταῖς καρδίαις ἡμῶν.

δοὺς τὸν ἀρραβῶνα τοῦ πνεύματος, also in v. 5; as in Ro. viii. 23, gen. of apposition.

ἀρραβών, cf. Eph. i. 14 similarly of τὸ πνεῦμα τὸ ἅγιον and with ἐσφραγίσθητε, associated with baptism. Also Papp., Inscrr.

For the 'giving' of the Spirit, cf. Ac. ii. 38 etc.

σφραγίζειν, fig., cf. Ro. xv. 28; Eph. i. 13, iv. 30; cf. J. iii. 33, vi. 27.

ἐν ταῖς καρδίαις, cf. Ro. v. 5; also 'indwelling,' Ro. viii. 9; 1 Cor. iii. 16.

249. ii. 13 οὐκ ἔσχηκα ἄνεσιν τῷ πνεύματί μου τῷ μὴ εὑρεῖν με Τίτον τὸν ἀδελφόν μου.

Cf. in idea 1 Cor. xvi. 18, of the human spirit.

ἄνεσις, cf. vii. 5, viii. 13; Ac. xxiv. 23; 2 Th. i. 7 (fig.).

ἔσχηκα, as i. 9, vii. 5; Ro. v. 2, pf. in aorist sense.

250. iii. 3 ἐνγεγραμμένη οὐ μέλανι ἀλλὰ πνεύματι θεοῦ ζῶντος.

A picture of mingled contrasts. Ezekiel's words (xi. 19, xxxvi. 26) seem in the memory of the Apostle for the material (flesh, stone), while for the instrument the invisible πνεῦμα is contrasted with the visible and tangible μέλαν (2 J. 12 ; 3 J. 13) ; but the results of its influence in the members of the community are as plain as the writing on papyrus or parchment. Once again the end of the work of the Spirit is the same as that of Christ.

251, 252. iii. 6 οὐ γράμματος ἀλλὰ πνεύματος, τὸ γὰρ γράμμα ἀποκτείνει, τὸ δὲ πνεῦμα ζωοποιεῖ.

The general characteristic of the new order is the influence of God-given πνεῦμα, while that of the old was written ordinance (γράμμα), the one inducing a state of death, the other a state of life (τὸ πνεῦμα taking up the πνεῦμα of the previous sentence), the one external, the other internal.

Cf. contrast of τὸ πνεῦμα and ἡ σάρξ, in words attributed to Jesus, J. vi. 63.

ζωοποιεῖ, cf. 1 Cor. xv. 45 n.

253. iii. 8 (εἰ δὲ ἡ διακονία τοῦ θανάτου ἐν γράμμασιν ἐντετυπωμένη λίθοις ἐγενήθη ἐν δόξῃ)...πῶς οὐχὶ μᾶλλον ἡ διακονία τοῦ πνεύματος ἔσται ἐν δόξῃ ;

τοῦ θανάτου ἐν γράμμασιν, cf. v. 6 τὸ γὰρ γράμμα ἀποκτείνει.

διακ. τοῦ πνεύματος, because as in v. 6 πνεῦμα is the characteristic of the Apostolic as opposed to the Mosaic ministration.

διακονία, 12 times in this letter alone ; Luke uses 9 times ; Heb. and Apoc. once each.

ἔσται, the δόξα of the new covenant is inherent and continuous, cf. 18, hence the allusion seems hardly to be to the presence of the Shekinah in the congregation.

254, 255. iii. 17 ὁ δὲ κύριος τὸ πνεῦμά ἐστιν· οὗ δὲ τὸ πνεῦμα Κυρίου, ἐλευθερία.

God's redemptive operation is through Christ, yet through the Spirit.

The ἐπιστρέφειν πρὸς Κύριον originally of Moses (Ex. xxxiv. 34) is used of accepting the Gospel-message, i.e. turning to ὁ κύριος, Christ (cf. 16, 18), but this is the change from a dispensation with γράμμα as the dominant characteristic to one with πνεῦμα (6, 8 etc.), and in this way 'Lord' and 'Spirit' can be identified in function, and in the sphere of that Spirit rule, which is also Christ's (Κυρίου gen. of apposition, v. l. κύριον?), is liberty, not bondage, and so open reflexion without κάλυμμα.

256. iii. 18 ...κατοπτριζόμενοι τὴν αὐτὴν εἰκόνα μεταμορφούμεθα ἀπὸ δόξης εἰς δόξαν, καθάπερ ἀπὸ Κυρίου πνεύματος.

The difficulties of interpreting πνεῦμα in this chapter come to a climax here : perhaps 'from the Lord, i.e. the Spirit' is best (we may compare Ro. viii. 2 ; 1 Cor. vi. 17, xv. 45), but one wonders whether the subtle, almost Rabbinic thought (cf. 1 Cor. x.) in these passages has rendered even our best texts untrustworthy. ἀπό could well = ὑπό, but reflexion seems the ruling idea ; yet cf. Gal. iv. 19 μέχρις οὗ μορφωθῇ Χ. ἐν ὑμῖν.

κατοπτρίζεσθαι here only in N.T., not class. or LXX.

μεταμορφοῦσθαι, also lit. of Transfiguration, M. xvii. 2 ; Mk ix. 2 and, fig., Ro. xii. 2 μεταμορφοῦσθε τῇ ἀνακαινώσει τοῦ νοός.

We may be permitted to note that the identification in these verses is an identification solely in effect of operation, and that on, primarily, the inward life of men : we are hardly justified in assuming metaphysical definition when the context bears witness that it is the expression of practical Christian experience, and, closest of all, that of the Apostle himself.

The chief thought is of the contrast of 'ministration,' not of the essential identification of 'Persons.'

257. iv. 13 ἔχοντες δὲ τὸ αὐτὸ πνεῦμα τῆς πίστεως.

πνεῦμα here means frame of mind, or temperament, characterized by faith (quâ creditur) like to that displayed in the Psalmist's expression ἐπίϲτεγϲΑ, Διὸ ἐλάλΗϲΑ (cxv. 10 LXX.) : this seems preferable to taking πνεῦμα of the cause for the effect or manifestation, sc. πίστις.

For τὸ αὐτὸ πνεῦμα, though not identical in sense, cf. 1 Cor. xii. 4, 8, 9, 11.

258. v. 5 ὁ δὲ κατεργασάμενος ἡμᾶς εἰς αὐτὸ τοῦτο θεός, ὁ δοὺς ἡμῖν τὸν ἀρραβῶνα τοῦ πνεύματος.

As in i. 22 note, ἀρρ. frequent in Inscrr. etc. πνεῦμα is but the pledge, the end is ζωή; this pledge is from God, never from Christ, in Paul.

κατεργάζεσθαι, only 5 times outside Ro. and 2 Cor., but class., LXX.

259. vi. 6 ἐν χρηστότητι, ἐν πνεύματι ἁγίῳ, ἐν ἀγάπῃ ἀνυποκρίτῳ.

A series of circumstances is followed by a series of qualities which mark the life and conduct and teaching of a διάκονος θεοῦ. In such a context the mention of an eternal personal distinction in the Godhead would surely be out of place, and the inclusion at the close of the sentence of ἐν δυνάμει θεοῦ (one aspect of the bestowal of πνεῦμα ἅγιον in Apostolic activity) leads us rather to interpret of the divine influence operating in the believer, the cause being named rather than the effect : this will still hold if we translate 'a spirit that is holy.'

The Christ-like χρηστότης, the common πνεῦμα ἅγιον, the God-like ἀγάπη remind us of xiii. 13 below ; cf. also Gal. v. 22.

χρηστότης, only Paul (Ro. 5 times and Tit. iii. 4 of God; of the Christian here, Gal. v. 22 ; Col. iii. 12 ; ἐν Χριστῷ, Eph. ii. 7). Class. and LXX.

ἀνυπόκριτος, of love also Ro. xii. 9, of faith 1 Ti. i. 5 ; 2 Ti. i. 5. Cf. Ja. iii. 17 of ἡ ἄνωθεν σοφία, 1 P. i. 22 of φιλαδελφία. Not class. but LXX. (Wisd. v. 18 etc.).

260. vii. 1 καθαρίσωμεν ἑαυτοὺς ἀπὸ παντὸς μολυσμοῦ σαρκὸς καὶ πνεύματος.

σάρξ and πνεῦμα (objective gen.) to cover the whole personality that the μολυσμός (here only) of sin affects : cf. Col. ii. 5, and, for implied contrast with νοῦς, Ro. i. 28; Col. ii. 18; Eph. iv. 17.

The human π. is the sphere of operation of the Holy Spirit, and thereby the whole being is a shrine, 1 Cor. iii. 16.

261. vii. 13 ὅτι ἀναπέπαυται τὸ πνεῦμα αὐτοῦ ἀπὸ πάντων ὑμῶν.

Cf. 1 Cor. xvi. 18 ; 2 Cor. ii. 13 note, τὸ πνεῦμα as a part representative of the whole self.

ἀναπαύειν also 1 Cor. xvi. 18 ; Phlm. 7, 20 similarly.

ἀπό, cf. L. vii. 35, viii. 43 etc. now taking the place of ὑπό.

262. xi. 4 εἰ μὲν γὰρ ὁ ἐρχόμενος ἄλλον Ἰησοῦν κηρύσσει ὃν οὐκ ἐκηρύξαμεν, ἢ πνεῦμα ἕτερον λαμβάνετε ὃ οὐκ ἐλάβετε.

We have entered a different atmosphere, a letter probably earlier, stern in tone and full of irony. Unlike the 'spirit' received at the believer's baptism, this 'spirit' (judged by its effects) is so 'different in kind' that it is designated elsewhere by the Apostle as π. δουλείας εἰς φόβον (Ro. viii. 15), π. κατανύξεως (xi. 8), τὸ π. τοῦ κόσμου (1 Cor. ii. 12) : but the passage is imaginative, a severely sarcastic hypothesis, 'some other Jesus, some different spirit !'

263. xii. 18 οὐ τῷ αὐτῷ πνεύματι περιεπατήσαμεν ; οὐ τοῖς αὐτοῖς ἴχνεσιν ;

The context shows πνεῦμα in this verse to be plan of life, regulative principles of conduct, within, manifested in the external ἴχνη : though we may look behind the close association in conduct to the πνεῦμα of which both Paul and Titus were partakers. (Cf. iv. 13 etc.) For the simile, see Gal. v. 16 etc.

264. xiii. 13 ἡ χάρις τοῦ κυρίου Ἰησοῦ [Χριστοῦ] καὶ ἡ ἀγάπη τοῦ θεοῦ καὶ ἡ κοινωνία τοῦ ἁγίου πνεύματος μετὰ πάντων ὑμῶν.

κοινωνία, cf. 1 Cor. x. 16 *bis*, of Eucharistic food, 2 Cor. viii. 4; with our verse we may compare, though there anarthrous, Phil. ii. 1 εἴ τις οὖν παράκλησις ἐν Χριστῷ, εἴ τι παραμύθιον ἀγάπης, εἴ τις κοινωνία πνεύματος, where there is also a threefold coordination; and the exhortations to order and unity on the basis of the one Spirit in diverse manifestation (1 Cor. xii. 4 ff.; Eph. iv. 3 ff.).

τοῦ ἁγίου πνεύματος, cf. 1 Cor. once, Ac. 6 times, L. twice, M. once. This is usually regarded as one of the ' proof-texts ' of the doctrine of the Trinity, but the probably original meaning does not of necessity involve any definite and consciously intentioned statement of a doctrine of the Godhead from within : it would seem at the outset more easy to regard the first and second genitives as subjective, and τ. ἁγίου π. as objective, the partaking-in-common of the Spirit from God, and so holy, which the Apostle links so often with the initiatory rite of Church membership (cf. the interpretative liturgical gloss 'and gift'), and so is a further plea for unity (11).

But on the other hand, the repeated articles, and the formation of the sentence, seem to demand that all the genitives should be similarly taken, i.e. subjectively, marking the source of the χάρις, of the ἀγάπη, of the κοινωνία. God and Jesus are to us 'personal,' and it is reasonable to infer the same of the third that is coordinated ; and the source behind, the efficient cause of the manifestations corporate or otherwise, is always the Spirit of God in the last resort : the Spirit that interacts with the human spirit, making realizable both communion with God, and fellow-membership with man.

Galatians.

265, 266, 267. iii. 2 ἐξ ἔργων νόμου τὸ πνεῦμα ἐλάβετε ἢ ἐξ ἀκοῆς πίστεως; 3 οὕτως ἀνόητοί ἐστε; ἐναρξάμενοι πνεύματι νῦν σαρκὶ ἐπιτελεῖσθε;...5 ὁ οὖν ἐπιχορηγῶν ὑμῖν τὸ πνεῦμα καὶ ἐνεργῶν δυνάμεις ἐν ὑμῖν, ἐξ ἔργων νόμου ἢ ἐξ ἀκοῆς πίστεως;

The spirit-gift followed upon faith (and baptism) as opposed to being the result of fulfilling legal ordinances: this being the dispensation characterized by 'spirit,' the former by 'flesh' (cf. Ro. viii. *passim*). Further, the divine source of the free bestowal is emphasized (ὁ ἐπιχορηγῶν), as well as the human reception (ἐλάβετε) ἐξ ἀκοῆς πίστεως. Cf. 14; Ro. viii. 15; 1 Cor. ii. 12; 2 Cor. xi. 4.

τὸ πνεῦμα and δύναμις associated (cf. Ac. xiii. 9 etc.).

τὸ πνεῦμα without qualification, as 2 Cor. i. 22, v. 5.

268. iii. 14 ἵνα τὴν ἐπαγγελίαν τοῦ πνεύματος λάβωμεν διὰ τῆς πίστεως.

τοῦ πνεύματος, gen. of apposition, as that in which the fulfilment consists (cf. Ac. ii. 33; Ro. viii. 23).

λαμβάνειν τὴν ἐπαγγ., cf. Ac. i. 4 (περιμένειν), ii. 33; Heb. ix. 15, vi. 15 (τυγχάνειν τῆς ἐπ.).

διὰ τῆς πίστεως, cf. ἐξ ἀκοῆς πίστεως iii. 2, 5 above. Faith is also a prerequisite for the Christian.

269. iv. 6 ἐξαπέστειλεν ὁ θεὸς τὸ πνεῦμα τοῦ υἱοῦ αὐτοῦ εἰς τὰς καρδίας ἡμῶν.

The thought of the passage leads us to compare Ro. viii. 14 ff., which regards π. rather from the side of the reception than of the mission as here. Since the believers are ἐν Χριστῷ, the π. υἱοθεσίας may be spoken of as τὸ πνεῦμα τοῦ υἱοῦ αὐτοῦ: cf. Ro. viii. 9 ff.; the effect is the same, but may be viewed from different standpoints.

ἐξαποστέλλειν, of the Son's mission (4), else Luke only

(Gosp. thrice, Ac. 7 times). We may contrast ἐκβάλλειν, ἐκπέμπειν by the Spirit, Mk i. 12 ; Ac. xiii. 4.

For ἡ καρδία as the sphere of the Spirit's operation, cf. 2 Cor. i. 22, iii. 3 ; Ro. v. 5, ii. 29, viii. 27 : as in Ps. seat of the inmost religious life.

270. iv. 29 ἀλλ' ὥσπερ τότε ὁ κατὰ σάρκα γεννηθεὶς ἐδίωκε τὸν κατὰ πνεῦμα, οὕτως καὶ νῦν.

κατὰ σάρκα...κατὰ πνεῦμα, cf. Ro. i. 3, viii. 4 etc.

For birth κατὰ πνεῦμα, we may cf. Jo. iii. 5 ff., M. i. 18 with different meanings. In this somewhat subtle and allegorical argumentation, Ishmael and the Judaizers stand over against the true Jews and the Christian Church, κατὰ σάρκα distinct from διὰ τῆς ἐπαγγελίας (23) or κατὰ πνεῦμα.

271. v. 5 ἡμεῖς γὰρ πνεύματι ἐκ πίστεως ἐλπίδα δικαιοσύνης ἀπεκδεχόμεθα.

There seems to be a tacit contrast with σαρκί lying in ἐν νόμῳ (4, 17), cf. iii. 2–5, while ἐκ πίστεως suggests ἐξ ἔργων νόμου in that passage.

ἐλπίς, not the act or state, but the object of hope, which consists in δικαιοσύνη (gen. of apposition).

ἀπεκδέχεσθαι, Ro. viii. 19, 23 ; 1 Cor. i. 7 (ἀποκάλυψις); Phil. iii. 20 (σωτήρ); Heb. ix. 28 (Χριστός). Without object, Ro. viii. 25 ; 1 P. iii. 20.

272, 273, 274. v. 16 πνεύματι περιπατεῖτε καὶ ἐπιθυμίαν σαρκὸς οὐ μὴ τελέσητε. 17 ἡ δὲ σὰρξ ἐπιθυμεῖ κατὰ τοῦ πνεύματος, τὸ δὲ πνεῦμα κατὰ τῆς σαρκός.

πνεῦμα and σάρξ once again opposed.

πνεύματι, dative of manner or rule, the life being renewed and transformed under the operation of πνεῦμα. Ro. viii. 11 etc. shows that it is not human πνεῦμα as such, but under the divine Spirit's influence (cf. iii. 14, iv. 6 etc.), i.e. regenerate, the personal cause comes to view in the following verses.

275. v. 18 εἰ δὲ πνεύματι ἄγεσθε, οὐκ ἐστὲ ὑπὸ νόμον.

Cf. 16, πνεύματι περιπατεῖτε, and, for the renewed πνεῦμα in harmony with the divine Will as guiding principle (ἄγειν), Ro. viii. 14 π. θεοῦ ἄγονται.

ἄγειν, elsewhere in Paul only Ro. ii. 4, 1 Cor. xii. 2, 1 Th. iv. 14 and 2 Ti. iii. 6, iv. 11: cf., for the thought, ὑπὸ χάριν εἶναι Ro. vi. 14.

νόμος interchanging with σάρξ, as ἐπαγγελία with πνεῦμα, in the contrast of life under the law and the Gospel: cf. iii. 17, iv. 5, v. 23. Although the phraseology is ambiguous, the personal agent becomes more prominent.

276. v. 22 ὁ δὲ καρπὸς τοῦ πνεύματός ἐστιν ἀγάπη, χαρά, εἰρήνη,....

The series of qualities marking the effect in the life of the new man in Christ can be designated καρπός as a sign of ζωή, while τὰ ἔργα τῆς σαρκός (19) tend to θάνατος; cf. Ro. viii. 6, vi. 21 etc., also 1 P. iii. 4.

Here most prominently the Spirit is the dominant factor in the continually developing ethical and religious experience of the individual. Though the scene of operation is the human life, the divine Spirit is the efficient cause.

277, 278. v. 25 εἰ ζῶμεν πνεύματι, πνεύματι καὶ στοιχῶμεν.

Cf. 16, 18, σάρξ being in the background here as well (τὴν σάρκα ἐσταύρωσαν, 24). If the dative has the same meaning both times, the clauses would seem to be too little distinguished: we may compare rather Ro. vi. 11 ζῶντας τῷ θεῷ; on the other hand, Ro. vi. 2, 10 τῇ ἁμαρτίᾳ ἀποθανεῖν, and so take the former πνεύματι as dat. of relation or respect, the latter as in v. 16 etc. dative of rule or manner.

πνεῦμα in all these cases with the fuller implication, the divinely given πνεῦμα indwelling and transforming the human.

στοιχεῖν, also Ac. xxi. 24 ; Ro. iv. 12 ; Gal. vi. 16 ; Phil. iii. 16, the last two with κανόνι expressed or understood.

Paul has various modes of expression for the same experience: the life that the Christian realizes is ἐν Χριστῷ, and yet Christ is the life (Col. iii. 4). The πνεῦμα is normative in the Christian's life, cf. also Ro. viii. 13, yet it is the πνεῦμα of the Father, who is Lifegiver as well (Ro. viii. 11).

279. vi. 1 ὑμεῖς δὲ πνευματικοὶ καταρτίζετε τὸν τοιοῦτον ἐν πνεύματι πραΰτητος.

πνεῦμα πραΰτητος, 1 Cor. iv. 21, gen. of definition or character ; cf. also v. 23, 1 P. iii. 4.

The πνευματικός in Paul is always the man in whom the divinely-given Spirit is the ruling principle, through his spirit progressively transforming him.

καταρτίζειν, cf. 1 Cor. i. 10; 2 Cor. xiii. 11; Heb. xiii. 21, class., LXX.

280, 281. vi. 8 ὁ δὲ σπείρων εἰς τὸ πνεῦμα ἐκ τοῦ πνεύματος θερίσει ζωὴν αἰώνιον.

εἰς τὴν σάρκα...εἰς τὸ πνεῦμα in familiar contrast.

The figure is bold, the metaphorical σπείρειν (of actions) falls into immaterial soil (πνεῦμα) and therefrom is reaped— the cornfield picture being inadequate—life eternal. The divine Spirit is in the thought the second time, for ζωή is ever God's gift, and the Spirit is source of the Christian's new life (Ro. viii. 2 etc.).

282. vi. 18 ἡ χάρις τοῦ Κυρίου [ἡμῶν] Ἰησοῦ Χριστοῦ μετὰ τοῦ πνεύματος ὑμῶν, ἀδελφοί, ἀμήν.

μετὰ τοῦ π., Phlm. 25, and 2 Ti. iv. 22. Cf. as well 2 Cor. ii. 13 (Paul), vii. 13 (Titus), where the πνεῦμα, the highest aspect, stands for the man, the whole personality.

ἀδελφοί, the word of gentle peace which turns the wrath away.

Ephesians.

283. i. 13 ἐσφραγίσθητε τῷ πνεύματι τῆς ἐπαγγελίας τῷ ἁγίῳ.

σφραγίζειν, cf. 2 Cor. i. 22 with δοὺς τὸν ἀρραβῶνα τοῦ πνεύματος (cf. *v.* 14), also Gal. iii. 14 τὴν ἐπαγγελίαν τοῦ πνεύματος; cf. Ac. i. 4.

τὸ πνεῦμα τὸ ἅγιον in Paul, iv. 30; 1 Th. iv. 8 (qu.), σφραγίζειν of πνεῦμα, also iv. 30.

The Spirit possessed by the Christian, and promised of old, is both pledge and portion of the glorious heritage. Here the separation lends emphasis to τῷ ἁγίῳ.

284. i. 17 ἵνα ὁ θεὸς τοῦ κυρίου Ἰησοῦ Χριστοῦ, ὁ πατὴρ τῆς δόξης, δῴη ὑμῖν πνεῦμα σοφίας καὶ ἀποκαλύψεως....

πνεῦμα σοφίας, cf. Gal. vi. 1 note, one aspect (or aspects, if ἀποκάλυψις is treated as a separate characteristic) of the gift of πνεῦμα, manifest in various developments according to the Church's need; giving a closer definition of εὐλογία πνευματικῇ (3), and looking forward in ἀποκαλύψεως to the μυστήριον of iii. 4 ff.

For connexion of σοφία with divine πνεῦμα, see En. xlix. 3; Wisd. i. 6, vii. 7, 22 (**A**, identified with π.), ix. 17 etc.; cf. Ps. Sol. xviii. 8. In a more charismatic sense, Ac. vi. 10.

[**285.** ii. 2 κατὰ τὸν ἄρχοντα τῆς ἐξουσίας τοῦ ἀέρος, τοῦ πνεύματος τοῦ νῦν ἐνεργοῦντος ἐν τοῖς υἱοῖς τῆς ἀπειθίας.]

In this difficult text, it seems simplest to suppose τοῦ πνεύματος attracted by the preceding genitives and, as if τὸ πνεῦμα, really in apposition with τὸν ἄρχοντα: τῆς ἐξουσίας will be object, and the ruler is Satan, as prince of evil spirits, who work in men, according to Paul's Jewish thought, as minions of an adverse power: cf. Mk iii. 22, J. xii. 31, 2 Cor.

iv. 4; cf. Eph. vi. 12 etc. For angels of spirits of natural phenomena, cf. Jub. ii. 2; and for evil powers over the same, Mart. Isa. ii. 2 ff., Test. Benj. iii. (τοῦ ἀερίου πνεύματος τοῦ βελίαρ prob.). If τοῦ π. refer to τῆς ἐξ. cf. 1 Cor. ii. 12.

286. ii. 18 ὅτι δι' αὐτοῦ ἔχομεν τὴν προσαγωγὴν οἱ ἀμφότεροι ἐν ἑνὶ πνεύματι πρὸς τὸν πατέρα.

ἐν πνεῦμα, the common disposition of prayer, itself the effect of the ἐν πνεῦμα bestowed alike on Jew and Gentile. The unity in Christ's body (16) is balanced by the union through one spirit, as a body of citizens or parts of a building (19 ff.).

προσαγωγή, also iii. 12; Ro. v. 2 : class.

Cf. Ignatius' curious figure, Eph. ix. 1; behind the disposition is the personal Source, as the triple coordination (Son—Spirit—Father) shows; cf. perhaps i. 17.

287. ii. 22 ἐν ᾧ καὶ ὑμεῖς συνοικοδομεῖσθε εἰς κατοικητήριον τοῦ θεοῦ ἐν πνεύματι.

πνεύματι, anarthrous after ἐν, but best taken as referring to the unifying Spirit, through whom the divine κατοίκησις takes place; nor is it to be forgotten that even the 'building together' is by the power and help of the divine Spirit, as shown by the expressions iii. 5, v. 18, vi. 18; so ἐν πνεύματι must be more than a descriptive qualification of κατοικητήριον.

συνοικοδομεῖν, here only in N.T., class.

κατοικητήριον, Apoc. xviii. 2 also, LXX.

288. iii. 5 ἀπεκαλύφθη τοῖς ἁγίοις ἀποστόλοις αὐτοῦ καὶ προφήταις ἐν πνεύματι.

ἐν πνεύματι marks the manner of ἀποκάλυψις to the Christian prophets; it was the same Holy Spirit that guided the unveiling of the old mystery in the new age (νῦν). If ἁγίοις be original with ἀποστόλοις, it is unique in Paul, cf. 1 Cor. xii. 28; Eph. iv. 11 etc.: the difficulty was felt; B om. ἀποστόλοις, so ps.-Ambrose also, while the Arm. tr. of Ephraem's

Comm. om. ἁγίοις and implies ἁγίῳ with πνεύματι, which would be more Pauline. But Col. i. 26 is clear with τοῖς ἁγ. αὐτοῦ and antecedent θεοῦ in 25. Eph. as it stands is hard to reconcile with Paul's story of his mission. προφῆται, 1, 2 Cor., Eph., Apoc. and Ac. frequently.

289. iii. 16 …δυνάμει κραταιωθῆναι διὰ τοῦ πνεύματος αὐτοῦ εἰς τὸν ἔσω ἄνθρωπον.

For the association of δύναμις and πνεῦμα on the inner ethical side, cf. 1 Cor. ii. 4 f.; Ro. xv. 13; 2 Ti. i. 7.

κραταιοῦσθαι with πνεύματι, L. i. 80, ii. 40, abs. 1 Cor. xvi. 13, also LXX.

The divine origin is emphasized (αὐτοῦ), and within the human πνεῦμα He has His sphere of working (εἰς τὸν ἔσω ἄνθρωπον); cf. Ro. vii. 22 κατὰ τὸν ἔσω ἄνθρωπον, 2 Cor. iv. 16 ὁ ἔσω ἡμῶν ἀνακαινοῦται, also 1 Pet. iii. 4 ὁ κρυπτὸς τῆς καρδίας ἄνθρωπος. This inward, continual and ethical operation of the Spirit is almost wholly Pauline.

290, 291. iv. 3 σπουδάζοντες τηρεῖν τὴν ἑνότητα τοῦ πνεύματος ἐν τῷ συνδέσμῳ τῆς εἰρήνης· 4 ἓν σῶμα καὶ ἓν πνεῦμα.

τοῦ πνεύματος, subjective, arising from the one Spirit; cf. 2 Cor. xiii. 13. ἑνότης, here and 13 also, class.; cf. ii. 18 ff.

σύνδεσμος, also Col. ii. 19, of ἀγάπη iii. 14, of ἀδικία Ac. viii. 23.

The meanings of the one Spirit indwelling the Church and of the πνεῦμα vivifying the σῶμα shade into one another; the Spirit is source of unity, yet also that in which it consists, in the Body of Christ. Cf. the argument on behalf of unity, 1 Cor. xii. 4 ff., the one 'body' with many 'members' whose renewed natures are vivified by the one Spirit of which each receives.

Eph. extends the idea of indwelling to the aggregate, the Church.

292. iv. 23 ἀνανεοῦσθαι δὲ τῷ πνεύματι τοῦ νοὸς ὑμῶν.

ἀνανεοῦσθαι, only here in N.T., class., LXX.

τῷ πνεύματι here defines the sphere of continual renewal (we might expect ἐν), unlike that of τὰ ἔθνη, 17.

νοῦς, probably here possess. gen., expresses the intellectual aspect of the higher nature of the individual, as in Ro. vii. 23, 25, xii. 2 (ἀνακαίνωσις); while it is contrasted with πνεῦμα 1 Cor. xiv. 14 f., and Col. ii. 18 is ascribed to the σάρξ.

293. iv. 30 καὶ μὴ λυπεῖτε τὸ πνεῦμα τὸ ἅγιον τοῦ θεοῦ, ἐν ᾧ ἐσφραγίσθητε.

τ. π. τ. ἅ., not else exactly in P.: cf. i. 13 (separated), 1 Th. iv. 8 (quotation); the thought is somewhat of a development.

λυπεῖν similarly, Herm. Mand. x. i. 2.   σφραγ., cf. i. 13.

To break the unity is to grieve the producer of it, cf. Ac. v. 3 f.; Is. lxiii. 10 ?

294. v. 18 καὶ μὴ μεθύσκεσθε οἴνῳ, ἐν ᾧ ἐστιν ἀσωτία, ἀλλὰ πληροῦσθε ἐν πνεύματι.

ἐν πνεύματι, rather of the sphere or organ of filling (as opposed to σάρξ implied in μεθύσκεσθε οἴνῳ), not of material. But the meaning is doublesided; the divine πνεῦμα works in and through the human, so if the chief thought be thereof, the dat. would be instrumental; cf. ii. 22.

μεθύσκειν, class., LXX., in N.T. L. xii. 45; J. ii. 10; 1 Th. v. 7; Apoc. xvii. 2.

ἀσωτία, also Tit. i. 6; 1 P. iv. 4, class., LXX.

295, 296. vi. 17 καὶ τὴν μάχαιραν τοῦ πνεύματος, ὅ ἐστιν ῥῆμα θεοῦ, 18 διὰ πάσης προσευχῆς καὶ δεήσεως, προσευχόμενοι ἐν παντὶ καιρῷ ἐν πνεύματι,...

τοῦ πνεύματος, gen. of origin or ownership, regarded as author of Scripture, the ῥῆμα θεοῦ; the πνεῦμα representative of the Deity, source of inspiration; cf. Is. xi. 4, L. iii. 2.

ἐν πν. denotes the manner of the προσεύχεσθαι, as ἐν παντὶ καιρῷ the time (cf. 1 Th. v. 17 ἀδιαλείπτως): but if Jude 20 (ἐν πνεύματι ἁγίῳ) be regarded as parallel, the dative will designate sphere or influence, rather than instrument; for the Spirit is continually the atmosphere as well as the help of the Christian's life, Ro. viii. 26 etc.

This possibility of a twofold sense for ἐν πνεύματι in Eph. renders certain interpretation difficult, as we cannot differentiate instrument and sphere by the mere absence or presence of ἐν.

Philippians.

297. i. 19 ...διὰ τῆς ὑμῶν δεήσεως καὶ ἐπιχορηγίας τοῦ πνεύματος Ἰησοῦ Χριστοῦ.

ἐπιχορηγία, and in Eph. iv. 16 ; cf. Gal. iii. 5 (ὁ οὖν ἐπιχορηγῶν ὑμῖν τὸ πνεῦμα), suggesting that Ἰησοῦ Χριστοῦ is gen. not of origin or possessor, but of character or definition, cf. Ac. xvi. 7 ; Ro. viii. 9 ; Gal. iv. 6, in Paul the Spirit being never sent by Christ.

τοῦ πνεύματος seems to be regarded as objective, yet at the same time the supplier is 'the Spirit of God,' which is 'the Spirit of (Jesus) Christ': cf. Ro. viii. 9.

298. i. 27 ὅτι στήκετε ἐν ἑνὶ πνεύματι, μιᾷ ψυχῇ συναθλοῦντες....

Cf. στήκετε ἐν Κυρίῳ, iv. 1.

It is possible to take πνεῦμα of the cause, but rather preferable of the effect which the one divine influence produces, spiritual agreement, one frame of mind ; this seems favoured by the immediately following μιᾷ ψυχῇ : if the former, cf. Eph. iv. 3, 4 ; Phil. ii. 1.

For ψυχή parallel with πνεῦμα, see L. i. 46, 47 and the extra-canonical literature.

299. ii. 1 εἴ τι παραμύθιον ἀγάπης, εἴ τις κοινωνία πνεύματος.

Combining with the opening words εἴ τις οὖν παράκλησις ἐν

Χριστῷ, we may compare 2 Cor. xiii. 13 (Christ, God's love, Spirit); but if one connects the thought with i. 27 and ii. 2 πνεῦμα will refer not to the divine gift but to the human mind, sc. 'spiritual sympathy' (σύνψυχοι, τὸ ἓν φρονοῦντες ii. 2).

παραμύθιον, here only, but cf. 1 Cor. xiv. 3 παράκλησιν καὶ παραμυθίαν from the Christian prophet. The phrase is ambiguous: π. may define the 'fellowship' or mark its source, as probably in 2 Cor.

300. iii. 3 ἡμεῖς γάρ ἐσμεν ἡ περιτομή, οἱ πνεύματι θεοῦ λατρεύοντες....

θεῷ ‫א‬ᶜD*P etc. ς, cf. Ro. i. 9, ὁ θεὸς ᾧ λατρεύω ἐν τῷ πνεύματί μου, and thus πνεύματι is here instrumental, with an implied opposition to σάρξ, the idea of which is contained in περιτομή.

If θεοῦ read, as best attested, then λατρεύειν must be used absolutely, and θεοῦ gen. of origin: while there will still be the contrast between the carnal ordinances and the spiritual (present) dispensation, cf. Ro. xii. 1 (λογικὴ λατρεία). π. θ. in Paul 9 times (τ. π. (τ.) θ. inclusive).

301. iv. 23 ἡ χάρις τοῦ κυρίου Ἰησοῦ Χριστοῦ μετὰ τοῦ πνεύματος ὑμῶν.

So also Gal. vi. 18, Phlm. 25; cf. 2 Ti. iv. 22, ὁ κύριος μετὰ τοῦ πνεύματός σου. ἡ χάρις μεθ' ὑμῶν.

The nobler part is named to represent the whole being.

Colossians.

302. i. 8 ὁ καὶ δηλώσας ἡμῖν τὴν ὑμῶν ἀγάπην ἐν πνεύματι.

The ἀγάπη of which Epaphras bore witness was in the sphere of spirit, i.e. πνευματική: ὑμῶν naturally being subjective, for ἐν σαρκί (ii. 5) they had not seen one another. Yet the God-given Spirit has 'love' for its firstfruit, so we

may not lose sight of the divine influence through the human;
ἐν πνεύματι even when the divine aspect is prominent being
almost always anarthrous in Paul, unless stylistic reasons
prevent: cf. 1 Cor. xii. 9.

303.   ii. 5 ἀλλὰ τῷ πνεύματι σὺν ὑμῖν εἰμί.

Compare 1 Cor. v. 3, ἀπὼν τῷ σώματι, παρὼν δὲ τῷ πνεύματι,
while here the protasis is εἰ γὰρ καὶ τῇ σαρκὶ ἄπειμι.
For the antithesis of πνεῦμα and σάρξ, see 1 Ti. iii. 16 etc.
The meaning is similar in 1 Th. ii. 17 (προσώπῳ οὐ καρδίᾳ).

1 Thessalonians.

304, 305.   i. 5 ὅτι τὸ εὐαγγέλιον ἡμῶν οὐκ ἐγενήθη
εἰς ὑμᾶς ἐν λόγῳ μόνον, ἀλλὰ καὶ ἐν δυνάμει καὶ ἐν
πνεύματι ἁγίῳ καὶ πληροφορίᾳ πολλῇ...6 καὶ ὑμεῖς...
δεξάμενοι τὸν λόγον ἐν θλίψει πολλῇ μετὰ χαρᾶς
πνεύματος ἁγίου.

πνεῦμα ἅγιον here of the divine influence which produces
in the Christian χαρά, even ἐν θλίψει πολλῇ, as one of its
effects.

For the combination of λόγος, δύναμις, πνεῦμα cf. 1 Cor. ii. 4.

δύναμις co-related with or dependent on πνεῦμα, Ro. xv.
13, 19 etc.; Gal. iii. 5.

πληροφορία, in Paul Col. ii. 2 also: elsewhere Heb. vi. 11,
x. 22; not class. or LXX., though the vb occurs: cf. Clem.
1 Cor. xlii. 3 μετὰ πληροφορίας π. ἁγίου.

χαρὰ πνεύματος ἁγίου, gen. of origin; cf. also χαρὰ ἐν πνεύματι ἁγίῳ, Ro. xiv. 17; Ac. xiii. 52.

With εὐαγγέλιον...ἐν π. ἁ., cf. 1 P. i. 12, the same Spirit
operates in both speaker and hearers.

Here, in one of the earliest examples of Pauline usage,
π. ἅ. is ethical rather than abnormal in effect, lasting rather
than occasional: cf. Gal. v. 16 ff., iii. 14 (where also linked
with faith), in a letter possibly earlier.

306. iv. 8 τοιγαροῦν ὁ ἀθετῶν οὐκ ἄνθρωπον ἀθετεῖ ἀλλὰ τὸν θεὸν τὸν διδόντα τὸ πνεῦμα αὐτοῦ τὸ ἅγιον εἰc ὑμᾶc.

Reminiscent of Ez. xxxvii. 14 καὶ δώσω τὸ πνεῦμα μου εἰς ὑμᾶς καὶ ζήσεσθε, of breath to dry bones, applied to the imparting of τὸ πνεῦμα τὸ ἅγιον : we might compare J. xx. 22 (ἐνεφύσησεν καὶ λέγει αὐτοῖς· λάβετε πνεῦμα ἅγιον), Ac. ii. 2–4. διδόντα (v. l. δόντα) of πνεῦμα ἅγιον etc., cf. Ac. v. 32.

Perhaps the insertion of τὸ ἅγιον is influenced by the dominant idea of ἁγιασμός (7), and distinguishes from the primary meaning 'breath.' Sanctification is a process (pres.).

τοιγαροῦν, here and Heb. xii. 1, but class., LXX.

ἀθετεῖν, in P. only 1 Cor. i. 19 (quoted); Gal. ii. 21 (grace), iii. 15 (covenant); 1 Ti. v. 12 (first faith): also Heb. x. 28; and Mk vi. 26, L. x. 16, J. xii. 48, Ju. 8, of persons.

307. v. 19 τὸ πνεῦμα μὴ σβέννυτε, προφητείας μὴ ἐξουθενεῖτε.

The commands of joy, prayer, thanks, are followed by two behests, each of a couplet, as it were, containing a general principle and special application tersely expressed.

τὸ πνεῦμα is the divine power of the primitive charismatic type in the believer in varied manifestations, of which προφητεία was one; the Thessalonians' caution is a contrast to the Corinthians' eagerness (1 Cor. xiv.), cf. Eph. iv. 30.

σβέννυτε, again in Mk ix. (44, 46), 48; M. xii. 20 (quot.), xxv. 8; Eph. vi. 16 (darts); Heb. xi. 34 (fire). Class., LXX.

ἐξουθενεῖν, only L. and Paul in N.T., LXX.

For the thought, cf. Ign. Polyc. ii. 2.

308. v. 23 καὶ ὁλόκληρον ὑμῶν τὸ πνεῦμα καὶ ἡ ψυχὴ καὶ τὸ σῶμα...τηρηθείη.

Paul neither treats of the salvation of the ψυχή, nor names it as representing the higher side of the human personality. Rather than technical (tripartite) definition, this is (as now) a popular designation of the whole man: cf. Heb. iv. 12, though not strictly parallel.

In Jewish apocalyptic we find ψυχή, or πνεῦμα, or both, named as persisting beyond death; but here, in the earliest expectation of the Apostle, the σῶμα also is preserved for the Parousia of Christ, cf. Ro. xii. 1; 1 Cor. vi. 19 f.

ὁλόκληρον, also Ja. i. 4 in N.T., class., LXX.

2 Thessalonians.

309. ii. 2 ...μηδὲ θροεῖσθαι μήτε διὰ πνεύματος μήτε διὰ λόγου....

Perhaps πνεύματος of the cause, when it is the manifestation or effect that is in mind; cf. 1 Th. v. 19. It must be a mode of communication which, like a spoken or written message, purported to come from the Apostle, in the (uncontrolled?) utterance of some brother.

Cf. such expressions not in agreement, Ac. xx. 22 f., xxi. 4, or the promptings of (evil) spirits (1 Tim. iv. 1); such phenomena therefore required discernment, 1 Cor. xii. 10, itself a special gift of the one Spirit.

πνεύματος, anarthrous, of the nature of the communication.

θροεῖσθαι, only Mk xiii. 7 ‖ M. xxiv. 6, class., LXX.

310. ii. 8 ὃν ὁ κύριος ['Ἰησοῦς] ἀνελεῖ τῷ ΠΝΕΥΜΑΤΙ τοῦ ΣΤΟΜΑΤΟΣ ΑΥΤΟΥ.

Cf. Is. xi. 4, καὶ πατάξει γῆν τῷ λόγῳ τοῦ στόματος αὐτοῦ καὶ ἐν (τῷ ℵ) πνεύματι διὰ χειλέων ἀνελεῖ ἀσεβῆ; and, for the breath of יהוה, symbolic of physical power, Hos. vi. 5; Ps. xxxii. 6: Apoc. xix. 15, 21 of the ῥομφαία out of Christ's mouth.

The following words (τῇ ἐπιφανείᾳ τῆς παρουσίας αὐτοῦ) make us recall the Jewish conceptions of divine self-manifestation in Memra and Shekinah.

311. ii. 13 εἰς σωτηρίαν ἐν ἁγιασμῷ πνεύματος καὶ πίστει ἀληθείας.

For the connexion of πνεῦμα and ἁγιασμός, cf. 1 Th. iv. 3–8.

The salvation consists in and through sanctification and faith, the one due to the working of the πνεῦμα (subjective gen.), the other having for its object ἀλήθεια (12). It is to be noted that 1 P. i. 2 has ἐν ἁγιασμῷ πνεύματος also, where θεοῦ πατρός, πνεύματος, Ἰησοῦ Χριστοῦ follow in order. The Holy Spirit begins the process.

ἁγιασμός, LXX., and besides Paul (8 times), Heb. xii. 14 ; 1 P. i. 2, in N.T.

1 *Timothy.*

312. iii. 16 ὃς ἐφανερώθη ἐν σαρκί,
              ἐδικαιώθη ἐν πνεύματι.

This parallelism (probably hymnal) leads us to think of Ro. i. 3 f. κατὰ σάρκα...κατὰ πνεῦμα, as also of 1 P. iii. 18 θανατωθεὶς μὲν σαρκί, ζωσποιηθεὶς δὲ πνεύματι, where the aspect is more narrow. The human πνεῦμα of the Incarnate Christ it is that persists, and in the sphere of spirit the authority, teaching etc. of the earth-manifestation receive their justification.

δικαιοῦν, only here pass. of Christ, though of God Ro. iii. 4 (qu. Ps. l. 6 LXX.); cf. L. vii. 35 ‖ M. xi. 19 of ἡ σοφία. The Pauline technical, forensic, sense is out of place here.

313, 314. iv. 1 τὸ δὲ πνεῦμα ῥητῶς λέγει...
[προσέχοντες πνεύμασι πλάνοις.]

τὸ πνεῦμα, either as author of a scripture (canonical or apocryphal) to us unknown; or, rather, as cause of some 'spiritual' utterance on the part of a 'prophetic' member of the community (cf. Ac. xi. 12, 28 etc.).

πνεύμασι will apparently refer to 'evil' spirits or their effects in the misleading speakers; cf. Col. i. 13; Eph. vi. 12 etc.; also 1 J. iv. 3, 6, 2 J. 7.

ῥητῶς, not elsewhere in N.T., post-class.

2 *Timothy*.

315. i. 7 οὐ γὰρ ἔδωκεν ἡμῖν ὁ θεὸς πνεῦμα δειλίας.

A disposition whose characteristic is δειλία is not the outcome of a divine gift; cf. Ro. viii. 2, 15; 2 Cor. iv. 13; Eph. i. 17. The bestowal is regarded as a whole (*v.* 6 τὸ χάρισμα), and seems to be associated as much, or perhaps more, with post-baptismal 'laying on of hands' as with 'ordination' (cf. 14).

δειλία, not else N.T., class., LXX.

δύναμις, closely connected, as Ro. xv. 13 etc.; here the characteristics of the divine operation are ethical (ἀγάπη and σωφρονισμός), and πνεῦμα, whose nature is described, anarthrous.

316. i. 14 τὴν καλὴν παραθήκην φύλαξον διὰ πνεύματος ἁγίου τοῦ ἐνοικοῦντος ἐν ἡμῖν.

It seems preferable to regard πνεῦμα ἅγιον, as in Ro. viii. 11, as the God-given influence rather than as personal: in the Christian this presence is normal and abiding.

καλός is a striking feature in the Pastorals: twice as many times as in the rest of the Pauline writings.

παραθήκη, only in Past. 1 Ti. vi. 20, 2 Ti. i. 12, 14; more than a credal form merely, the 'deposit' of Apostolic preaching.

317. iv. 22 ὁ κύριος μετὰ τοῦ πνεύματός σου.

Compare the close in Gal. vi. 18, Phlm. 25; here the 'grace' is reserved for wider greeting (ὑμῶν) than the primary addressee.

Probably the copyists were right to refer the title here to Jesus in spiritual presence.

For the fuller τοῦ πνεύματός σου, cf. Phlm. 25; Gal. vi. 18; Phil. iv. 23; also Barn. xxi. 9.

Titus.

318. iii. 5 διὰ λουτροῦ παλινγενεσίας καὶ ἀνακαινώσεως πνεύματος ἁγίου.

The accompanying circumstances of σωτηρία, and both

associated with the λουτρόν of baptism.   Gen. of description
rather than of apposition.   The clause is a compendium of
Pauline thoughts.   λουτρόν, Eph. v. 26; cf. Heb. x. 22.
παλινγενεσία, although only in M. xix. 28 else, is in harmony with the teaching of baptismal symbolism, Ro. vi.;
J. iii. 3 ff. etc.   ἀνακαίνωσις, Ro. xii. 2 (ἀν. τοῦ νοός) also,
by the continual operation in the believer of πνεῦμα ἅγιον,
received at or immediately after the entrance rite, a result
distinctly inward and ethical; cf. 2 Cor. vi. 6, Ac. ii. 38.

Philemon.

319.   25 ἡ χάρις τοῦ κυρίου Ἰησοῦ Χριστοῦ μετὰ τοῦ
πνεύματος ὑμῶν.

Cf. Gal. vi. 18; 2 Ti. iv. 22.

The form, apart from τοῦ πνεύματος, is according to the
type of conclusion in the earlier letters.

§ 6.   Johannine Writings.

S. John.

320.   i. 32 τεθέαμαι τὸ πνεῦμα καταβαῖνον ὡς
περιστερὰν ἐξ οὐρανοῦ.

τὸ π. καταβαῖνον ὡς περιστεράν, cf. Mk i. 10 ∥.

τεθέαμαι, pf. also 1 J. iv. 12, θεὸν οὐδεὶς πώποτε τεθέαται,
14 καὶ ἡμεῖς τεθεάμεθα καὶ μαρτυροῦμεν ὅτι...

It is noteworthy that in J. it is to the Baptist that the
vision of the Spirit's descent is accorded.   A Jew would hardly
use (originally) (א)רוח unqualified, cf. L. iii. 22, but to the
Christian the expression was sufficiently definite.

321, 322.   i. 33 ἐφ' ὃν ἂν ἴδῃς τὸ πνεῦμα καταβαῖνον
καὶ μένον ἐπ' αὐτόν, οὗτός ἐστιν ὁ βαπτίζων ἐν πνεύματι
ἁγίῳ.

βαπτίζειν ἐν πν. ἁγ.   Mk i. 8, M. iii. 11, L. iii. 16;
Ac. i. 5, xi. 16, passive.

καὶ μένον, taking up καὶ ἔμεινεν, 32, the emphasis upon permanent possession of the Spirit—for the disciples also— being especially Johannine, while the unique endowment of the Messiah is again prominent, cf. Synn., En., Ps. Sol., Test. Patr., even to the words which express His message (vi. 63).

323. iii. 5 ἐὰν μή τις γεννηθῇ ἐξ ὕδατος καὶ πνεύματος, οὐ δύναται....

Water is not named again in the context; Syr. Sin. reads 'of the Spirit and water,' and Just. Ap. I. 61 does not refer to ὕδατος καί. Yet water typifies Spirit iv. 10 ff., vii. 38. The saying is sacramental, if anticipatory (cf. xx. 22): it suggests Church experience of the illapse of the Spirit at baptism as the source of new life, cf. i. 33, Tit. iii. 5.

324, 325. iii. 6 καὶ τὸ γεγεννημένον ἐκ τοῦ πνεύματος πνεῦμά ἐστιν.

For ἐκ cf. 5, 8, γεγεννημένον 8 also.

Only in these verses do we meet just this conception of birth from the Spirit, elsewhere it is of God, i. 13, viii. 47 (cf. vi. 65), as in 1 J.; and J. never in any way identifies the Father and the Spirit. With this idea of separateness of flesh- and spirit-life, without divine intervention, there is a similarity of thought in the contrast of divine and human sonship in M. i. 18, L. i. 35.

πνεῦμα, anarthrous, as marking the nature belonging to the heavenly order, akin to that of the origin of all regenerate life, cf. Syr. Sin. addn, 'because God is a living Spirit.' Ign. Phil. vii. 1, though not a real parallel, deserves comparison, εἰ γὰρ καὶ κατὰ σάρκα μέ τινες ἠθέλησαν πλανῆσαι, ἀλλὰ τὸ πνεῦμα οὐ πλανᾶται, ἀπὸ θεοῦ ὄν.

326, 327. iii. 8 τὸ πνεῦμα ὅπου θέλει πνεῖ,...οὕτως ἐστὶν πᾶς ὁ γεγεννημένος ἐκ τοῦ πνεύματος.

This seems to revert to the older view of the divine Spirit as mysterious, powerful, occasional like the wind, absolute in operation, and (cf. Paul) giving freedom to those 'born from' it (cf. 6). Personification applies to both meanings; perhaps the idea of divine Breath links the two aspects of birth.

א, O.L., O. Syr., etc., add ὕδατος καί here, cf. 5.

It must be admitted that this line of thought is absent from the Synoptic teaching attributed to Jesus.

328. iii. 34 οὐ γὰρ ἐκ μέτρου δίδωσιν τὸ πνεῦμα.

If, as is most in keeping with the context, God is the donor and the Son, the Messiah, the recipient, the verse is in agreement with later Jewish doctrine of Messianic endowment. If the thought be wider, it is still in harmony with the belief that the Spirit-gift is unaffected in its fulness by distribution, cf. Bammidbar Rabba 15.

μέτρον, 14 times in N.T., here only ἐκ μέτρου.

δίδωσιν, sc. the Father, xiv. 26, xv. 26, cf. Ac. and Paul. For the contrast of the partial with this perfect correspondence with the divine Will, cf. 1 Cor. xiii. 9 f., Col. i. 19.

329, 330, 331. iv. 23 ὅτε οἱ ἀληθινοὶ προσκυνηταὶ προσκυνήσουσιν τῷ πατρὶ ἐν πνεύματι καὶ ἀληθείᾳ... 24 πνεῦμα ὁ θεός, καὶ τοὺς προσκυνοῦντας αὐτὸν ἐν πνεύματι καὶ ἀληθείᾳ δεῖ προσκυνεῖν.

ἐν πνεύματι, here almost adverbial; the worship must emanate from that part of man's being most akin to the divine, for God the Father's essential nature is spirit. This is the distinctly 'mystic' doctrine of direct access and direct communion, apart from the charismatic ecstasy of the prophet or even birth from water and the Spirit, and apart from all material accessories. πνεῦμα as God in operation is always ἅγιον, because holiness is an attribute of His essential nature, although Greek writers (e.g. Paul) did not need always to express it, as the Jews did (רוח קדשא, etc., cf. Targums).

προσκυνηταί, only here: P. uses προσκυνεῖν but once (1 Cor. xiv. 25), and then of the outward prostration (as 23), rather than of this richer 'spiritually' reverential worship (acc. 24).

332, 333. vi. 63 τὸ πνεῦμά ἐστιν τὸ ζωοποιοῦν,...τὰ ῥήματα ἃ ἐγὼ λελάληκα ὑμῖν πνεῦμά ἐστιν καὶ ζωή ἐστιν.

The Spirit of God is the source of life and the begetter of the new life within man, cf. iii. 6: the contrast here goes deeper than the usual anthropological antithesis of πνεῦμα and σάρξ. The utterances of Jesus as a vehicle of that divine influence partake of the nature of spirit and so of life, and they are abiding also in their effect (λελάληκα), cf. i. 33, iii. 34.

We may compare this intimate relationship in activity of Christ and the Spirit with the interchange of subject in Apoc. ii. 1, 7, etc., where the function too is revealing (λέγει). A kindred line of thought is manifest in Paul, Ro. viii. 2, 2 Cor. iii. 6 (π. ζωῆς, π. ζωοποιεῖ), cf. Gal. v. 25 (εἰ ζῶμεν πνεύματι), etc.

The physical basis of the simile is emphasized in Syr. Sin. by the addition of 'the body' as object. For the distinctness of the spiritual order, cf. iii. 6.

334, 335. vii. 39 τοῦτο δὲ εἶπεν περὶ τοῦ πνεύματος οὗ ἔμελλον λαμβάνειν οἱ πιστεύσαντες εἰς αὐτόν· οὔπω γὰρ ἦν πνεῦμα ὅτι Ἰησοῦς οὔπω ἐδοξάσθη.

In this author's comment, we have the first mention of the Spirit as a bestowal on all believers, a conception which figures largely in the last discourses. οὔπω...ἐδοξάσθη might be secondary, compared with the narrative xx. 22, unless the 'glorification' be regarded by the writer as completed at the Resurrection; though xx. 17 implies, as M. Ac., some preparatory process, at least relatively to man ; and xvi. 14, etc. it is the Spirit that 'glorifies' Christ: at any rate, this second clause has suffered in transmission by the addition of ἅγιον or δεδομένον or both.

Spirit, manifest as bestowed on the Church for witness, etc., not in essential nature non-existent before. The teaching of the first portion is similar to that of the farewell address, bodily presence renders spiritual presence unnecessary. The

glorification of the Son by the Father is characteristic of this
Gospel, yet He is glorified by the Spirit (xvi. 14), and the
Father by the Son (xvii. 4) ; but the thought is absent from
the Apocalypse, for the already glorified Jesus is Revealer.
This explanation of 38 (ποταμοὶ...ὕδατος ζῶντος) reminds us
of ποταμὸν ὕδατος ζωῆς in the vision of the descending City
(Ap. xxii. 1). When we consider this doctrine and that of
cc. xv.–xvii. esp., we seem forced to regard that of iii. 5 ff. as
proleptic, if reminiscent of actual converse.

336. xi. 33 (Ἰησοῦς) ἐνεβριμήσατο τῷ πνεύματι
καὶ ἐτάραξεν ἑαυτόν.

τὸ πνεῦμα marks the sphere of the 'groaning,' the inward
human spirit is the subject of emotion, cf. xiii. 21 (xix. 30),
Mk ii. 8, viii. 12, (L. x. 21), Ac. xvii. 16, etc. It is somewhat
uncertain whether, in the view of the author, the lack of hope
and confidence (32, 37), or sympathy with the suffering that
death brings, prompted this 'self-troubling.'

ἐμβριμᾶσθαι, also 38, M. ix. 30, Mk i. 43, xiv. 5.

ταράσσειν, 6 times in Gosp., reflexive only here, but cf.
xii. 27 (soul), xiii. 21 (spirit) ; 9 times elsewhere.

337. xiii. 21 ταῦτα εἰπὼν Ἰησοῦς ἐταράχθη τῷ
πνεύματι καὶ ἐμαρτύρησεν....

Here, as opposed to xi. 33, it is the personal agony of a
crisis that is the cause of the intense feeling which is manifested in a sad μαρτυρία concerning betrayal. The self-troubling
is again localized in the πνεῦμα of Jesus. As always in J.,
μαρτυρεῖν used in words ascribed to the incarnate Word has a
doctrinal significance, testimony to some religious 'truth' concerning Himself or His mission, through Himself or the Spirit.

338. xiv. 17 ἄλλον παράκλητον δώσει ὑμῖν ἵνα ᾖ
μεθ᾽ ὑμῶν εἰς τὸν αἰῶνα, τὸ πνεῦμα τῆς ἀληθείας.

τὸ πνεῦμα τῆς ἀληθείας, cf. xv. 26, xvi. 13, 1 J. iv. 6 ;
the prophetic spirit that comes into Rebekah's mouth is called
'spirit of truth' Jub. xxv. 14, cf. Test. Judah xx., in contrast

to spirit of error witnessing in human conscience : such is out-poured, too, by Messiah, Test. Jud. xxiv., Levi xviii.

ἄλλος, but another mode of Christ's presence to their spirits, yet contrast ἔρχομαι πρὸς ὑμᾶς (18) : again τὸ π. is a gift (δώσει) not occasional but constant, as always in J.

ἀλήθεια characterizes on one side the nature of the Spirit, on another the result of the operating, sc. knowledge concerning the Incarnate Logos : perhaps cf. π. σοφίας καὶ ἀποκαλύψεως of Paul. παράκλητος, 26, xv. 26, xvi. 7; 1 J. ii. 1 of Christ.

339. xiv. 26 ὁ δὲ παράκλητος, τὸ πνεῦμα τὸ ἅγιον ὃ πέμψει ὁ πατήρ....

The Spirit 'sent' by the Father, or 'given' (17) is one personal mode of His self-revealing to men, just as was the 'sending' of the Logos, and here too the knowledge of the truth of that revelation is the special aspect emphasized (διδάξει, ὑπομνήσει), cf. 17, xvi. 13, 1 J. iv. 6, v. 6. πέμψει, of God, yet πέμψω of Christ xv. 26, xvi. 7, cf. xx. 22, while xvi. 13 the Spirit 'comes'; so the twin views cross and recross. The old idea of witness through the Apostles (Mk xiii. 11, etc.) is given more permanent validity, while J.'s forms of expression are more mystical; in such a way the mind of Christ is so realized within that the content of His message is gradually revealed.

340. xv. 26 ὅταν ἔλθῃ ὁ παράκλητος ὃν ἐγὼ πέμψω ὑμῖν παρὰ τοῦ πατρός, τὸ πνεῦμα τῆς ἀληθείας ὃ παρὰ τοῦ πατρὸς ἐκπορεύεται.

πέμψω, cf. xiv. 26, L. xxiv. 49 ἐξαποστέλλω τὴν ἐπαγγελίαν τοῦ πατρός μου, Ac. ii. 33. τ. π. τῆς ἀλ. xiv. 17, n.

ὅταν, specially Johannine (17 times), also 1 J. v. 2, Apoc. 9 times, etc.

παρὰ τοῦ πατρός, cf. i. 14 μονογενὴς παρὰ πατρός, yet Christ comes Himself (xiv. 18) and the Spirit from Him (xvi. 7); indeed also, supposing Gospel and Epistle to be of the same author and time, πρὸς τὸν πατέρα Jesus Christ is Paraclete (1 J. ii. 1), but πρὸς τοὺς ἀνθρώπους the Spirit (J. not 1 J.).

ἐκπορεύεται seems strange; the comp. only v. 29 else
in J., but the simple vb sometimes used of the Son (xvi. 7).
This sending and going forth of the Spirit must be identified
apparently with the coming of Jesus xiv. 17 f.

341. xvi. 13 ὅταν δὲ ἔλθῃ ἐκεῖνος, τὸ πνεῦμα τῆς
ἀληθείας, ὁδηγήσει ὑμᾶς εἰς τὴν ἀλήθειαν πᾶσαν.

For the wording, cf. xiv. 17, xv. 26 above.

To the Spirit of truth are ascribed thus personal activities
of which the O.T. has no trace (ἀκούει, λαλήσει, ἀναγγελεῖ, etc.),
but are only attributed to Jahweh : as if, though unexpressed
in so many words, the Spirit too is θεός, is πρὸς τὸν θεόν (i. 1).
ὁδηγεῖν, else M. xv. 14 = L. vi. 39, Ac. viii. 31, Ap. vii. 17 ;
and this guidance by its very definition is regarded as continuous
and not intermittent.

342. xix. 30 καὶ κλίνας τὴν κεφαλὴν παρέδωκεν
τὸ πνεῦμα.

As M. xxvii. 50, Ac. vii. 59 the God-given principle of
life, symbolized by, and of old identified with, the breath,
departing at death.

κλίνειν, M. viii. 20 = L. ix. 58 (sleep), xxiv. 5 (faces), ix. 12,
xxiv. 29 (ἡμέρα), Heb. xi. 34 ; not sleep, but rest in the Father
after finished work seems thought of here (cf. Abbott, Joh.
Vocab. 9 ff.). παρέδωκεν also marks the free volition of the
act more clearly than Mk, L. (ἐξέπνευσεν) or M. (ἀφῆκεν τ. π.),
in harmony with the Pauline παραδόντος ἑαυτόν Gal. ii. 20,
παρέδωκεν Eph. v. 2, 25, and the kingly demeanour of Jesus
through the whole Gospel ; cf. the purposefulness of Jesus'
outbursts of emotion, such M. for reverence eliminates.

343. xx. 22 καὶ τοῦτο εἰπὼν ἐνεφύσησεν καὶ λέγει
αὐτοῖς Λάβετε πνεῦμα ἅγιον.

ἐμφυσᾶν, here only, cf. metaphor iii. 8, Ac. ii. 2 ff.,
illustrating the close connexion in thought as well as word
of 'breath' and 'Spirit' (iii. 8, vi. 63). Cf. Gen. ii. 7 LXX.

πνεῦμα ἅγιον, as nowhere else in J., cf. Ac. i. 2, etc.

Is this episode narrated in compensation for the less mystical phenomena recounted Ac. ii. ? Can it be said to agree with the conception of the Spirit's 'mission' xv. 26, xvi. 7 ? The action is sacramental; be this the founding or no, the Church is a new creation. λάβετε, xiv. 16, vii. 39; the Spirit is received by the disciples (after the Resurrection), and continues in them (the Church) the same God-revealing activity as did the Logos in the flesh.

1 S. John.

344. iii. 24 καὶ ἐν τούτῳ γινώσκομεν ὅτι μένει ἐν ἡμῖν, ἐκ τοῦ πνεύματος οὗ ἡμῖν ἔδωκεν.

The manifestation of the Spirit-gift in life is the evidence of the Christian's mystical union with God, ἐν αὐτῷ...ἐν αὐτῷ, ἐν ἡμῖν, and so τὸ πνεῦμα is in a way the source (ἐκ) of his γινώσκειν that God abides in the Church (ἡμῖν): cf. J. xiv. 23.

For τὸ πνεῦμα definitely stated as 'given,' cf. Ac. v. 32, viii. 18, xv. 8, 2 Cor. i. 22, without ἅγιον in 1 J., Apoc. The source is given, but it is the proof, the effect in life, that is strictly the ground of knowledge : cf. Paul's connexion of the Spirit and sonship, Ro. viii., etc.

345, 346. iv. 1 ἀγαπητοί, μὴ παντὶ πνεύματι πιστεύετε, ἀλλὰ δοκιμάζετε τὰ πνεύματα εἰ ἐκ τοῦ θεοῦ ἐστιν.

The quasi-personification need not be pressed, it is the distinction of truth from falsehood in teaching and confession that is essential, and the test is belief in a real incarnation (2), cf. aim of Gospel, xx. 31. The πνεῦμα in this and the following verse practically = the human individual through whom the Spirit is manifested, although the attention is fixed on the good or evil impulse to whose influence his 'prophecy' or 'confession' is attributed.

δοκιμάζειν, cf. L. xii. 56, 1 Th. v. 21, Ro. xii. 2, 1 Cor. xi.

28, xvi. 3, 2 Cor. viii. 8, 22, xiii. 5, Gal. vi. 4, Eph. v. 10, 1 Ti. iii. 10.

For misleading 'prophesying,' cf. Apoc. ii. 20, 2 P. ii. 1, M. xxiv. 11.

347, 348, 349. iv. 2 ἐν τούτῳ γινώσκετε τὸ πνεῦμα τοῦ θεοῦ· πᾶν πνεῦμα ὃ ὁμολογεῖ Ἰησοῦν Χριστὸν ἐν σαρκὶ ἐληλυθότα ἐκ τοῦ θεοῦ ἐστιν, 3 [καὶ πᾶν πνεῦμα ὃ μὴ ὁμολογεῖ....]

The test is general, as the confession or non-confession is repeated and continuous (pres.). πᾶν πνεῦμα, as in 1, in both cases comes to mean 'everybody who,' cf. ii. 22, 23.

τὸ πν., i.e. the manifestation of the Spirit which is God-given (gen. of source) is the object of perception ; as is also that of τὸ (πνεῦμα) τοῦ ἀντιχρίστου (3) by non-confession of the Incarnation.

ὁμολογεῖν, cf. ii. 23, iv. 15 (ὅτι), 2 J. 7 (ptc.). J. xii. 42 (abs.).

For further signs of testing, ethical or confessional, cf. Herm. Mand. xi. 7 (ἀπὸ τῆς ζωῆς, πραΰς), Did. xi. 8, etc.

350, 351. iv. 6 ἐκ τούτου γινώσκομεν τὸ πνεῦμα τῆς ἀληθείας καὶ [τὸ πνεῦμα τῆς πλάνης].

The contrast of ἀλήθεια and πλάνη runs through all these verses.

τὸ πνεῦμα τῆς ἀληθείας, such is ἄλλον παράκλητον in J. xiv. 16, 17.

τὸ πνεῦμα τῆς πλάνης, only here ; but in Paul, for ἡ πλάνη, cf. 1 Th. ii. 3, 2 Th. ii. 11 (ἐνέργειαν πλ.), Eph. iv. 14.

Compare also Test. Reub. ii. (7 sp. of error), Judah xx. (sp. of truth and sp. of error with man), xxiv. (sp. of truth outpoured), En. lvi. 5, Ps. Sol. viii. 15, Asc. Isa. iii. 28, cf. 1 Ti. iv. 1.

352. iv. 13 ὅτι ἐκ τοῦ πνεύματος αὐτοῦ δέδωκεν ἡμῖν.

τὸ πνεῦμα is now the gift bestowed at the outset of the Christian's career (iii. 24 ἔδωκεν), now the inexhaustible fount of grace, from which the Christian goes on drawing continually (ἐκ, δέδωκεν) according to need, and using according to capacity in the Church, and which is the token of a mutual 'abiding'; contrast J. iii. 34 of Christ. It is possible that this gift is designated χρίσμα in ii. 20, 27, but not connected with Baptism.

353, 354. v. 6 καὶ τὸ πνεῦμά ἐστιν τὸ μαρτυροῦν, ὅτι τὸ πνεῦμά ἐστιν ἡ ἀλήθεια.

Jesus Christ came once for all (ὁ ἐλθών), but the work of witness which belongs to τὸ πνεῦμα is continuous (μαρτυροῦν), and, rather than predicating truth of the witness, τὸ πνεῦμα is itself identified with ἡ ἀλήθεια; cf. J. xiv. 6 ἐγώ εἰμι ἡ ὁδὸς καὶ ἡ ἀλήθεια καὶ ἡ ζωή. ἡ ἀλήθεια is most prominent in the Johannine writings, but is absent from the Apocalypse, where, however, cf. xix. 10 for a close connexion of μαρτυρία and πνεῦμα.

These references (iv. 6, J. xiv. 26, xvi. 13), identifying truth with, or attributing it to, the Spirit, show how the inward and ethical view has become predominant over the earlier external and occasional: cf. 1 Cor. ii. 11.

355. v. 8 ὅτι τρεῖς εἰσιν οἱ μαρτυροῦντες, τὸ πνεῦμα καὶ τὸ ὕδωρ καὶ τὸ αἷμα, καὶ οἱ τρεῖς εἰς τὸ ἕν εἰσιν.

τὸ πνεῦμα, the witness to the glorified Christ within the believers, τὸ ὕδωρ that of the Baptism, τὸ αἷμα that of the Death, combining to assure the reality of the Incarnation, as opposed to Docetic theories, cf. iv. 2 f., J. xix. 34, etc., or it may be the internal yet eternal and unseen witness behind and through and combined with the outward rites of Baptism and Eucharist that is in the writer's mind, cf. J. iii. 5, vi. 53, etc.

In all these passages we have some aspect of God in operation, and therefore a divine personal continuing amongst men —all other operation has passed from the horizon of N.T. thought—of the work of the incarnate Logos; yet from the human standpoint conceived as a gift received by the

Christian community and so by its individual members, and that, as with Paul, normal and continual, rather than startling and occasional in effect, making especially for growth in knowledge, in perception of (Christological) truth.

Here we may note that πνεῦμα with any connotation is absent from 2 and 3 John: it is also remarkable that the attribute ἅγιον meets us in none of the Johannine works, except Gosp. xx. 22, and this tends to indicate non-Jewish readers.

Apocalypse.

356. i. 4 καὶ ἀπὸ τῶν ἑπτὰ πνευμάτων ἃ ἐνώπιον τοῦ θρόνου αὐτοῦ.

The seven spirits, also iii. 1 (ὁ ἔχων . .), iv. 5 (ἑπτὰ λαμπάδες... ἅ εἰσιν . .), v. 6 (ἀρνίον...ἔχων...ὀφθαλμοὺς ἑπτά, οἵ εἰσιν . .), cf. the seven stars, i. 16, 20, ii. 1, iii. 1 in the hand of the divine Christ, called angels, viii. 12 ; so also cf. Tob. xii. 15, En. xc. 21 f., Test. Levi viii. for seven angel-ministers, and the seven star-gods of Babylonian religion, etc.

The word ἐνώπιον arrests us ; it is predominantly Lucan (Gosp. 21, Ac. 13 times) outside this book (35 times), and the Epp. to Timothy (8 times). Very frequent in LXX. for לִפְנֵי, also Papp. and Inscrr., cf. Tg. Onk. on Gen. i. 2. Can we then interpret these passages in Apoc. of the sevenfold opera-tion of the Third Person of the Everblessed and Undivided Trinity ? Not at least primarily, it would be an anachronism, and it does not suit the context ; ἐνώπιον, λαμπάδες, ὀφθαλμοί all plainly imply service rather than equality, activities not essence, leading us to regard the expressions as material of vision-language, as in Zech. iv., Ez. i., etc., signifying the completeness of revelation through Christ. For 'the throne' practically meaning God, cf. Ap. Bar. xlvi. 4, Life of Adam xxxii., etc.

We may be permitted to think that in Apocalyptic sym-bolism and mystic numbers such as these we should recognize

imagery from Jewish speculation etc., not fully assimilated to
the Christian standpoint of the work as a whole, if indeed it
does not incorporate existing material.

357. i. 10 ἐγενόμην ἐν πνεύματι ἐν τῆ κυριακῆ
ἡμέρα.

ἐν πνεύματι, also iv. 2 (ἐγενόμην), xvii. 3, xxi. 10
(ἀπήνεγκέν με) ; with the last cf. the Pauline ἁρπαγέντα . . ἕως
τρίτου οὐρανοῦ (2 Cor. xii. 2), and Ac. viii. 39. For this
expression to signify the state of prophetic rapture, cf. En.
lxxi. 5, also Ez. iii. 14, xxxvii. 1, here only (i. 10, iv. 2)
absolutely in N.T., cf. Herm., Vis. I. i. 3, II. i. 1.

κυριακός, 1 Cor. xi. 20 (δεῖπνον) else, Inscrr., etc., cf.
Did. xiv., κυριακὴ κυρίου, of the first day of the week, not the
'day of the Lord,' for the vision is for the present encouragement of suffering churches.

Such usage of ἐν πνεύματι leads us back to the conceptions
of early Jewish-Christian days (Ac.), when the ecstatic and
prophetic was more prominent than the moral and abiding
aspect of the divine operation in men.

358. ii. 7. **359.** 11. **360.** 17. **361.** 29. **362.** iii. 6.
363. 13. **364.** 22 ὁ ἔχων οὖς ἀκουσάτω τί τὸ πνεῦμα
λέγει ταῖς ἐκκλησίαις.

Seven times verbatim. The solemn summons precedes the
promise which concludes the messages to Ephesus, Smyrna
(ii. 11), Pergamos (ii. 17), but follows in those to Thyateira
(ii. 29), Sardes (iii. 6), Philadelphia (iii. 13), Laodikia (iii. 22).

For the interpretation it is important to note the opening
of these Spirit-spoken messages : the speaker is described as
ὁ κρατῶν τοὺς ἑπτὰ ἀστέρας ἐν τῆ δεξιᾷ αὐτοῦ, ὁ περιπατῶν ἐν μέσῳ
τῶν ἑπτὰ λυχνιῶν τῶν χρυσῶν (ii. 1), ὁ πρῶτος καὶ ὁ ἔσχατος, ὃς
ἐγένετο νεκρὸς καὶ ἔζησεν (ii. 8), ὁ ἔχων τὴν ῥομφαίαν τὴν δίστομον
τὴν ὀξεῖαν (ii. 12), ὁ υἱὸς τοῦ θεοῦ, ὁ ἔχων τοὺς ὀφθαλμοὺς αὐτοῦ ὡς
φλόγα πυρός, καὶ οἱ πόδες αὐτοῦ ὅμοιοι χαλκολιβάνῳ (ii. 18), ὁ
ἔχων τὰ ἑπτὰ πνεύματα τοῦ θεοῦ καὶ τοὺς ἑπτὰ ἀστέρας (iii. 1),
ὁ ἅγιος, ὁ ἀληθινός, ὁ ἔχων τὴν κλεῖν Δαυείδ, ὁ ἀνοίγων καὶ οὐδεὶς

κλείσει, καὶ κλείων καὶ οὐδεὶς ἀνοίγει (iii. 7), ὁ ἀμήν, ὁ μάρτυς ὁ πιστὸς καὶ ἀληθινός, ἡ ἀρχὴ τῆς κτίσεως τοῦ θεοῦ (iii. 14); undoubtedly this is the incarnate and glorified Jesus Christ (i. 1), conceived as giving His revelation through the seer, who is himself ἐν πνεύματι (i. 10), and yet at the close of each message it is said to be that of the Spirit. Christ, therefore, and the Spirit are treated as being interchangeable as authors of the messages, apparently because both are modes of the operation of God amongst men in revelation, so for the seer's purpose it is immaterial whether Christ or the Spirit of God speaks through himself.

365. iii. 1 τάδε λέγει ὁ ἔχων τὰ ἑπτὰ πνεύματα τοῦ θεοῦ.

See i. 4, iv. 5 also.

God's power operative in revelation is in the hands of the glorified Christ: seven, as the Churches were seven; or, as occurring frequently in Apocalyptic literature and later speculation, like the 7 (or 6) 'Archangels,' En. xx., xc. 21, Tob. xii. 15 with their series of ministerial personifications, cf. i. 4.

366. iv. 2 μετὰ ταῦτα εὐθέως ἐγενόμην ἐν πνεύματι.

Cf. i. 10 of the prophetic state; cf. Ez. iii. 12 ff.

The seer is conceived as seized by a divine power which takes him out of his natural condition to view the heavenly throne, cf. i. 4, etc. Here we can compare Hebrew prophecy and Greek mantic; and to the Jew the demoniac in his ravings was also ἐν πνεύματι, but πνεύματι ἀκαθάρτῳ (Mc. i. 23, etc.).

367. iv. 5 καὶ ἑπτὰ λαμπάδες πυρὸς καιόμεναι ἐνώπιον τοῦ θρόνου, ἅ εἰσιν τὰ ἑπτὰ πνεύματα τοῦ θεοῦ.

Cf. i. 4., iii. 1, v. 6.

Probably Zech. iv. 2 (6) lies behind the prophet's symbolism of distributive revelation.

λαμπάs, also viii. 10, else only M. xxv., J. xviii. 3, Ac. xx. 8. For such ministerial agency of spirits in explanation of divine operation, cf. 3 Regn. xxii. 21, as well as these symbolic quasi-personifications in Zech. iv. The connexion with fire, light, etc., is noteworthy, cf. Ps. ciii. 4, Paul's 'angel of light,' En. li. 5, cviii. 11, etc.

368. v. 6 ἔχων...ὀφθαλμοὺς ἑπτά, οἵ εἰσιν τὰ [ἑπτὰ] πνεύματα τοῦ θεοῦ ἀπεσταλμένοι εἰς πᾶσαν τὴν γῆν.

Cf. iv. 5 above ; also Zech. iii. 9, iv. 10 'eyes of Jahweh.' Whether ἀπεσταλμένοι be original or not, the πνεύματα are clearly conceived as being ministerial, whether symbolized by λαμπάδες or ὀφθαλμοί, and as denoting God's power in revelation are in the hands (ἔχων) of the Ascended Lord, the Lamb once slain. Again ministerial agencies connected with light : was it thought to be angelic substance? Even the saints are so clothed, En. lxii. 16, Ap. Bar. li. 10.

369. xi. 11 καὶ μετὰ [τὰς] τρεῖς ἡμέρας καὶ ἥμισυ ΠΝΕΥΜΑ ζωῆς ἐκ τοῦ θεοῦ εἰϹΗΛΘΕΝ ἐΝ ΑΥτοῖϹ.

Reminiscent of Ez. xxxvii. 5, 10, which suggests 'breath' as the right rendering, cf. also Gen. ii. 7, or rather that which the breath symbolized, the power of physical life, which was ἐκ τοῦ θεοῦ.

For πνεῦμα ζωῆς, cf. Jud. xvi. 14, 4 Ezr. iii. 5, Ap. Bar. xxiii. 5, Sib. iv. 187, and Paul (Ro. viii. 2, etc.).

370. xiii. 15 καὶ ἐδόθη αὐτῇ δοῦναι πνεῦμα τῇ εἰκόνι τοῦ θηρίου.

πνεῦμα in this passage must be similar in sense to πνεῦμα ζωῆς xi. 11, contrast J. xix. 30. The 'breath' is the token of the life which manifests itself in speech (ἵνα καὶ λαλήσῃ), but the term is general and otherwise undefined, for, unlike the life-giving power in Creation (Gen. vi. 17, etc.), it is only indirectly from God.

371. xiv. 13 ναί, λέγει τὸ πνεῦμα, ἵνα ἀναπαήσονται ἐκ τῶν κόπων αὐτῶν.

Apparently, as in ii. 7, etc., the Spirit is used indifferently with Christ, so here, instead of the Christ without, it is the Spirit within responding and assuring the prophet: cf. xxii. 17.

ἀναπαύειν, cf. vi. 11, 1 Cor. xvi. 18, etc., and, for the thought of the rest of the righteous, Wisd. v. 5, etc.

κόπος, only in ii. 2, and 5 times in Gospp. outside Paul; here, too, unlike in Paul, ἔργα in a good sense to be remembered when κόποι are forgotten.

[**372, 373**. xvi. 13 καὶ ἐκ τοῦ στόματος τοῦ ψευδο-προφήτου πνεύματα τρία ἀκάθαρτα ὡς βάτραχοι· εἰσὶν γὰρ πνεύματα δαιμονίων ποιοῦντα σημεῖα.]

πνεῦμα ἀκάθαρτον, cf. Mk i. 23, etc., 2 Th. ii. 8 (with στόμα), conceived as materialised in the shape of frogs, βάτραχος occurring but here in N.T.

δαιμονίων probably gen. of apposition; here affecting men from without, as in 1 Tim. iv. 1, 1 J. iv. 3 from within.

σημεῖα, mostly the Fourth Gospel in this sense; also Ac., but nearly always in combination.

374. xvii. 3 καὶ ἀπήνεγκέν με εἰς ἔρημον ἐν πνεύματι.

For the phrase cf. xxi. 10, with ἐγενόμην i. 10, iv. 2. The Temptation commences in a similar manner, Mk i. 12 and parallels.

So also Ez. speaks of himself, xxxvii. 1 ἐξήγαγέν με ἐν πνεύματι Κύριος: cf. iii. 14 καὶ τὸ πνεῦμα ἐξῆρέν με καὶ ἀνέλαβέν με, καὶ ἐπορεύθην ἐν ὁρμῇ τοῦ πνεύματός μου, καὶ χεὶρ Κυρίου ἐγένετο ἐπ' ἐμὲ κραταιά, and iii. 12, viii. 3 (hand), xi. 24, sufficiently descriptive of the potency of the divine afflatus; cf. the more realistic seizure, Bel 36, and Gosp. Hebr. fr. 2, both by the hair.

[**375**. xviii. 2 καὶ ἐγένετο...φυλακὴ παντὸς πνεύ-ματος ἀκαθάρτου.]

πνεῦμα ἀκάθαρτον as in xvi. 13, reflecting the later Jewish view that ethnic deities were evil spirits.

φυλακή, of the abode of discarnate spirits of men, 1 Pet. iii. 19, not prison here, cf. Bar. iii. 34. For the thought we may compare the taunt-song in Is. (xiii. 21, cf. xxxiv. 11, 13), also Baruch iv. 35 καὶ κατοικηθήσεται ὑπὸ δαιμονίων τὸν πλείονα χρόνον, Tobit viii. 3 ὅτε δὲ ὠσφράνθη τὸ δαιμόνιον τῆς ὀσμῆς, ἔφυγεν εἰς τὰ ἀνώτατα Αἰγύπτου, καὶ ἔδησεν αὐτὸ ὁ ἄγγελος.

376. xix. 10 ἡ γὰρ μαρτυρία Ἰησοῦ ἐστὶν τὸ πνεῦμα τῆς προφητείας.

Having regard to the preceding words σύνδουλός σού εἰμι καὶ τῶν ἀδελφῶν σου τῶν ἐχόντων τὴν μαρτυρίαν Ἰησοῦ, as also to the fact that this book itself is called a 'prophecy' (xxii. 10), it seems best to take Ἰησοῦ and τῆς προφητείας as objective gens. μαρτυρία is a mark of the Christian prophets, among whom the writer ranks himself (xxii. 9), so τὸ πνεῦμα in this connexion must be used for the divine Spirit whose characteristic operation in the Church is προφητεία; within them is τ. π. τῆς προφητείας, without is the manifestation of that possession, μαρτυρία Ἰησοῦ, cf. Herm., Mand. xi. 9. If, however, Ἰησοῦ be subjective, it would throw light on the equivalence of the messages of Christ and the Spirit to the Churches; prophecy on earth and divine testimony agree.

377. xxi. 10 καὶ ἀπήνεγκέν με ἐν πνεύματι ἐπὶ ὄρος μέγα καὶ ὑψηλόν.

See xvii. 3 n., also i. 10, iv. 2. Ez. xl. 1, 2 καὶ ἤγαγέν με...καὶ ἔθηκέν με ἐπʼ ὄρος ὑψηλὸν σφόδρα, where ἐν ὁράσει θεοῦ takes the place of ἐν πνεύματι here for the prophetic rapture.

We may contrast the Temptation vision from an ὄρος ὑψηλόν M. iv. 8, and cf. the mythical mountain in the north, Isa. xiv. 13, etc.

378. xxii. 6 καὶ ὁ κύριος ὁ θεὸς τῶν πνευμάτων τῶν προφητῶν....

The inferior reading ἁγίων for πνευμάτων τῶν may be compared with that in 2 P. i. 21 (οἱ) ἅγιοι (τοῦ) θεοῦ ἄνθρωποι.

The expression is more emphatic than τῶν προφητῶν alone, for the part named is just that through which the prophet is influenced: for the human side, cf. esp. 1 Cor. xiv. 32 πνεύματα προφητῶν προφήταις ὑποτάσσεται. πνεῦμα as representative of the whole man, esp. in Paul's greetings, Gal. vi. 18, etc.

'Lord of spirits' reminds us of the frequent usage in Enoch, cf. Jubilees x. 3 'God of spirits,' also ὁ τῶν πνευμάτων καὶ πάσης ἐξουσίας δυνάστης of 2 Macc. iii. 24, but of course with a quite different meaning, spirits of angels or discarnate spirits of men.

379. xxii. 17 καὶ τὸ πνεῦμα καὶ ἡ νύμφη λέγουσιν· Ἔρχου.

Because (τὸ) πνεῦμα καὶ (ἡ) νύμφη cry in response to the words ἐγὼ Ἰησοῦς κ.τ.λ. in the previous verse, it must be the Spirit thought of as working in and through the human persecuted faithful : this is not really greatly different from the view in ii. 7, etc., where the message of the Spirit through the prophet ἐν πνεύματι is yet also that of the glorified Jesus, only here it is the reply of the spirit-filled on earth to the promise from heaven : so the Spirit is, somewhat as in Paul, the prayer-inspiring power, acting through the seer in the Church, the Bride of the glorified Lord, cf. the author's (?) prayer (20), and xiv. 13, xix. 10.

νύμφη, cf. xxi. 2, 9 of Ἰερουσαλὴμ καινή.

Ἔρχου, cf. ἔρχομαι ταχύ iii. 11, xxii. 7, 12, 20 ; and the closing petition of this sole representative of Christian 'prophecy' (i. 3, xxii. 10) in the N.T., ἔρχου, κύριε Ἰησοῦ.

§ 7. OUTLINE SURVEY.

It may be well to review the N.T. references in somewhat the same way as we have done those from the O.T. and extra-canonical writings.

After the separation from the mother Jewish Church, dating practically from the initial persecution in which Stephen suffered, it is but natural that the religious community that regarded the Crucified as Messiah should assume the position in the literature which the old nation and kingdom and Church had formerly occupied, especially after the Messianic endowment at Pentecost: thus the first section 'In Nation' now comes to have the further significance 'In the Christian Church,' so conscious of the present operation of the Holy Spirit in and through its members.

This affects the evidence throughout: it is the Christian believer supremely on or in whom the Spirit works, and it is the spirit of the Christian that is almost exclusively mentioned.

Gospels and Acts.

Divine Spirit.

A. In Nation (Christ's Kingdom, Church).

i. O.T. heroes. Mk xii. 36, Ac. i. 16 (David), Ac. xxviii. 25 (Isaiah).

ii. Preparers for Messiah. M. i. 18 (Mary), L. i. 41 (Elizabeth), 67 (Zacharias), 15 (John the Baptist).

iii. Messiah. Mk i. 8 ff., cf. iii. 29, Ac. i. 2, L. x. 21.

iv. Followers of Messiah—Apostles etc. continuing the work of the Incarnate Lord. Mk xiii. 11, L. xi. 13, Ac. i. 5, ii. 4, v. 32 (witness) etc.; x. 19, xiii. 2 (Spirit conceived as speaking).

B. In Man (Christian).

1. Occasional. Ac. ii. 4, x. 44 (glossolaly); xi. 28 (foretelling); viii. 29 (impulsive guidance); ii. 38 (given), xi. 15 (manifestly apparent in believers).

2. Permanent, seemingly with more lasting and ethical effect, Ac. vi. 3, 10 (intelligent capacity); vi. 5, xi. 24, ix. 31 (faith and comfort).

Some of these Church or individual references might change places, according to the standpoint from which they are regarded.

C. In World.

No trace now, God operates by Spirit-gift only in and through man, especially the Christian.

Spirit-being, L. xxiv. 37 ff., Ac. xxiii. 8 f.

[Evil-spirit, with or without ἀκάθαρτον, frequently: Mk i. 23, Ac. v. 16 etc.; πονηρόν, L. vii. 21 etc.]

Human Spirit.

(a) emotional, Mk ii. 8 (knowledge), viii. 12 (groaning); Ac. xvii. 16.

(b) volitional, Mk xiv. 38 (opp. σάρξ), Ac. xix. 21.

(c) personal, L. i. 47 (|| ψυχή), 80 (rational life). M. xxvii. 50, L. viii. 55 (life as given by and returned to God; also Ac. vii. 59).

Hebrews and Catholic Epistles.

Divine Spirit.

A. In Nation (Christ's Kingdom, Church).

i. O.T. writers. Heb. iii. 7 etc., 2 P. i. 21, 1 P. i. 11 (π. Χριστοῦ).

ii. Christ. Heb. ix. 14?

iii. Church. Apostles and faithful, Heb. ii. 4, vi. 4; 1 P. i. 2 (sanctification), 12; Ju. 19?

B. In Man.

1. Occasional (prayer), Ju. 20.

2. Permanent, Heb. vi. 4, Ja. iv. 5.

C. In World. No instance.

Spirit-beings, Heb. i. 7, 14, xii. 9? 1 P. iii. 19 (? fallen angels).

Human Spirit.

(a) emotional, no instance.

(b) volitional, disposition 1 P. iii. 4.

(c) personal, Heb. iv. 12, xii. 9, 23 (after death), 1 P. iii. 18 (opp. σάρξ), 19 (? discarnate men), Ja. ii. 26 (life-principle, opp. σῶμα).

In these writings the usage of πνεῦμα on the divine or human side is but sparing, and there is no striking development, the references to O.T. writers being of an early type, while Pauline influence may be found in the allusions to the imparting to believers.

Pauline Epistles.

Divine Spirit.

A. In Christ's Kingdom, the Church.

i. In O.T. writers. No direct allusion.

ii. The ministry of the Spirit is also Christ's, Ro. viii. 2 ? 2 Cor. iii. 17.

iii. Church. As aggregate of congregations and in-dividuals bound by one Spirit (Eph. iv. 4), imparted to all (iv. 30, 1 Cor. xii. 13).

Prophetic and administrative offices therein, though primarily individual, 1 Cor. xii.

B. In Man.

1. Occasional, 1 Cor. xii. (glossolaly), 1 Th. v. 19 (prophecy), Ro. viii. 26 (guidance).

2. Permanent, working normally in the believer's ordinary life, in most Epistles; this 'new' life is Spirit-caused, filled, helped etc. and is 'in the Spirit,' e.g. freedom-bringing Ro. viii. 2, prayer-helping viii. 26, teaching 2 Cor. ii. 13, sanctifying etc. 1 Cor. vi. 11, cf.

xiii. ἀγάπη the greatest of χαρίσματα: this use is the great development.

C. In World. None.

[Evil, Eph. ii. 2, 1 Ti. iv. 1.]

Human Spirit.

(a) emotional, Ro. xii. 11, 1 Cor. xvi. 18, 2 Cor. vii. 13.

(b) volitional, disposition Gal. vi. 1, Ro. viii. 15 ? 1 Cor. iv. 21; regenerate under divine influence Ro. viii. 16, Phil. i. 27 ? etc.

(c) personal, for 'self,' Gal. vi. 18, 1 Cor. v. 4, Phil. iv. 23, 2 Ti. iv. 22, Phlm. 25 ; after death Ro. i. 4, 1 Cor. xv. 45, 1 Ti. iii. 16 ; rational life 1 Cor. ii. 11 (divine analogue).

πνεῦμα opp. σάρξ Ro. viii. 4 etc., Gal. iii. 3.

    „   „ γράμμα Ro. ii. 29 etc.

    „   „ σῶμα 1 Th. v. 23 etc.

In Paul the connexion is so intimate and the language so much the reflexion of inner experience that it is very difficult often to separate the divine from the human aspect. To him each Christian is, or ought to be, πνευματικός.

Johannine Writings.

Divine Spirit.

A. In Nation (Kingdom, Church).

i. O.T. No instance.

ii. Christ. i. 32 f., iii. 34; cf. Sp. indifferently speaker with Christ, Apoc. ii. 7 etc.

iii. Church. Disciples, body of faithful, vii. 39, xx. 22 (general); xiv. 17, xv. 26, xvi. 13 (τ. π. τῆς ἀληθείας); 1 J. iii. 24, iv. 13 (indwelling), v. 8 (witnessing).

In heavenly vision, '7 spirits' as ministerial agency, Apoc. i. 4 etc.

B. In Man.

1. Occasional (prophetic ecstasy), Apoc. i. 10 etc.

2. Permanent (religious), J. iii. 5, 6, 8 (source of Christian's life).

C. In World. No reference.

Spirit-beings, Apoc. i. 4 etc.?

[Evil significance, Ap. xvi. 13 f., xviii. 2, 1 J. iv. 3, 6.]

Wind, J. iii. 8. Breath, Apoc. xi. 11, xiii. 15.

Human Spirit.

(a) emotional, J. xi. 33, xiii. 21.

(b) volitional, this aspect seems involved (for J.) in (a).

(c) personal (life principle), xix. 30, Apoc. xi. 11? cause for person, manifesting good or evil influence, 1 J. iv. 2?

In this part of the literature, the occurrences in the Apocalypse are more distinctly Jewish and more early in kind, with ministerial symbolism on the one hand, and prophetic experience on the other: while in the Gospel πνεῦμα expresses the nature of God (iv. 24), and is predicated of the message of Jesus (vi. 63); and in the Epistle we reach the identification of τὸ πνεῦμα with 'the truth' (v. 6).

A few references are thus set down at the close of the N.T. data arranged in outline classification in a similar manner to that of the introductory survey, thereby showing in some degree the contrast in development and usage.

We cannot help marking one great change from the

older Jewish conceptions, and it is this: the historic
past and the hope of the future alike recede in the N.T.
before the predominant present of personal and collective
Christian experience.

This change is plainly due to the two historic events,
intimately linked together, the Incarnation and Pentecost;
to the Apostolic writers the Spirit works in and through
the life of the Christ, and, after His departure, it is God's
—or Christ's—Spirit that sways and guides the young
communities in their early crises (Ac.), believers individually (Paul), and the Church corporately (John).

Following on the large increase of instances with the
'evil' shade of meaning that confronts us in the extra-
canonical literature arising from dualistic influences under
and after the Persian overlordship, we find in the N.T. evil
spirits spoken of chiefly in connexion with the wondrous
works of Jesus and the Apostles, coupled with the attribute of uncleanness, or some other typical of the disease
caused thereby, the reality of demonic agency being
unquestioned.

On the human side the wealth of reference is mainly
with Paul; here the $\pi\nu\epsilon\hat{\upsilon}\mu\alpha$ of man is so transformed and
regenerated by the operation of the Holy Spirit that it
assumes a higher meaning, as the organ of, or in a sense
being, the new nature in Christ, so under the divine
influence the guiding faculty of daily conduct; indeed,
so intimately connected are the divine and human sides
in Christian individual experience that it is sometimes
impossible to distinguish clearly which is primarily intended.

The old prophetic and ecstatic phenomena ascribed to
the heroes of early times were less in evidence between
the Testaments, but they meet us in ample richness in the

days of the infant Church both as glossolaly and as prophecy in the restricted sense, in the revelations experienced by a Paul, in the apocalyptic visions of a John.

But the transformation that is widest, and of most modern interest, is that of the view—no doubt finding responsive echoes among thoughtful members of the Apostolic congregations, but due at least in the development in which we find it before us to Paul's personal experience—of the Holy Spirit's presence in the spirit of the Christian disciple as a permanent indwelling, religious and ethical in effect. This belongs, however, to our Second Part, where we endeavour to gather together, though it be but inadequately, the teaching which the N.T. as it reaches us affords concerning that divine Spirit. The new life from its beginning is His operation, rather than only single episodes therein, the life of the Christian in the Church, the life whose noblest fruitage and whose surest test consist in that character and conduct after the pattern of the Incarnate, whose ruling feature is Love.

Conspectus of Distribution.

Bk	τ.π.	(evil)	π.	(evil)	π.ά.	τ.π.τ.ά.	τ.ά.π.	π.Κ.	τ.π.Κ.	π.θ.	τ.π.(τ.)θ.	π.X.	τ.π.I.	τ.π.I.X.	Total
Mk	5	9		5	1	3		1		1	τ.π.θ.1 / τ.π.τ.πατ.1				23
M.	6	2	1	2	3	1	1	1					1		19
L.	6	5	4	7	8	3	2								36
Ac.	15	5	3	3	18	17	6								70
Heb.	2		5		2	3	1								12
Ja.	1		1		1		1		1			τ.π.X.1			2
1 P.	1		4		1						τ.τ.θ.π.1				8
2 P.					1										1
Ju.			1												2
Ro.	15		10		6	(1+τ.θ.) 2				2	4	1		1	34
1 C.	20		12		1				1	2					40
2 C.	9		4		1					1					17
G.	10		8												18
E.	4	1	7	1	2	1				1					14
Ph.	1		2												5
Col.	1		1												2
1 Th.	2														5
2 Th.	1														3
1 T.	1		2		1										3
2 T.	1		1		1										3
Ti.			1												1
Phm.	1														1
J.	14	1	7	1	2	1					1				24
1 J.	7		2												12
Ap.	15		6	3											24
All N.T.	138	[23]	82	[22]	49	31	11	2	2	7	8	2	1	1	379

PART II.

THE HOLY SPIRIT AND HIS WORK.

§ 1. THE SYNOPTISTS.

THERE has been set forth already in the First Part, together with a brief amount of annotation, every sentence or portion of a sentence that contains the word 'spirit.' The inquiry was indeed originally begun in order to examine the contrast of 'flesh' and 'spirit' in the N.T. writings, but during the development of the investigation the centre of interest passed from the anthropological to the divine side, and widespread intercession in our land for 'a fresh outpouring of the Holy Spirit' only served to show that the study is not entirely out of touch with the thoughts and aspirations of our time.

For any understanding of the relation of the Spirit to man, to the individual and to the Christian Church, a humble and reverent examination of the earliest material at our disposal seemed to be imperative.

At this stage, therefore, we may set ourselves to discover what is the teaching which the fragmentary relics of the Christian literature of the first age afford us on the subject. To attempt anything more than a brief record of this information would lead us much too far afield, and to trace the development from the embryonic (divine) pneumatology of the writings to the philosophically worked-out pneumatology of the Catholic Church is the task of those who live beside broad streams of knowledge rather than of a solitary servant of the Church to whom hours of leisure are but very occasional.

If we desire to gather together the threads of the teaching, it is not unnatural that our earliest thought should be, What was the mind of the Master? How far did He give us any expression of His teaching upon the subject of our quest? This brings in turn a further question, What was the mind of the delineators of the portraits of Christ? In other words, there is incumbent upon us the delicate and difficult task of calling attention to any peculiarity of thought or diction on the subject on the part of the editor or compiler of material concerning the earthly life of Jesus, and also of taking into account the inevitable, indirect and unconscious effect of the modes of thought which were obtaining when the writings arose.

A perusal of the Synoptic references to $\pi\nu\epsilon\hat{\upsilon}\mu\alpha$ on the divine side leads us first to consider the relation of the Spirit to Jesus Himself, directly or indirectly. We may sum the data thus:

(a) Direct.

i. The Spirit is the instrument or medium of the Messianic Baptism. Mk i. 8 = M. iii. 11 = L. iii. 16.

ii. The descent of the Holy Spirit on Jesus at the Baptism, Mk implying a personal, M. and L. a more public, vision. Mk i. 10 = M. iii. 16 = L. iii. 22.

iii. The Spirit drives or leads Jesus to (and from, L.) the Temptation. Mk i. 12 = M. iv. 1 = L. iv. 1 (14).

iv. An Evangelist's comment by means of a witness from prophecy. M. xii. 18.

v. An indirect claim to personal fulfilment of prophecy on the part of Jesus. L. iv. 18.

vi. An Evangelist's comment as to Jesus' joy. L. x. 21.

The last three are peculiar to the respective compilers.

(b) Indirect. Previous to the Baptism.

i. Special endowment of John (L. i. 15, 17), of Mary (i. 35), Elizabeth (i. 41), Zacharias (i. 67) and Symeon (ii. 25 f.).

Following the incarnate life.

ii. A gift from the Father, personal, without limitation, but for the condition of asking. L. xi. 13 (peculiar, cf. M. vii. 11).

iii. Special and occasional assistance of the disciples in personal defence under legal process. Mk xiii. 11, M. x. 20, L. xii. 12, cf. xxi. 15, apparently out of connexion in Luke.

John the Baptist, it is to be noted, makes no claim to the possession of the Spirit himself in his work, just as we find the prophets of old did not do so for themselves, but later ages claimed it for them as for the heroes of ancient time. There is at least no public recognition of the details given in Luke concerning the special preparatory equipment of his parents or of the promise concerning himself (b, i.). This fact, at least as far as we have any report of his preaching of repentance, lends support to the contention that it was the refining fire of purification and of judgement that formed the contrast to water-baptism in the original form of the tradition (a, i.). It is in full accord with Jewish expectations, however, that the Messiah should have plenary endowment for his work (Mk i. 8), and the illapse of the Holy Spirit at the Baptism with its accompanying Palestinian symbolism finds a place in each of the records of the life of Jesus. But the variations in the narration are of moment as marking distinctions of points of sight on the part of the Gospel-writers; to Mark the accompanying vision is for Jesus, to M. and L. apparently for others also, to J. primarily as a witness for the Baptist to the person of the Messiah, although the Baptism itself is not recorded.

[Here we note, in parenthesis, that the throwing back of the 'anointing' of Jesus in the written records as time went on cannot be without some significance. The first confirmation, for the Apostles at least, of the Petrine confession concerning the Messiahship of Jesus seems to have been at the Transfiguration; then in the earliest Gospel we find the consecration for the earthly ministry is related in connexion with the Baptism, and first—as Jesus presumably recounted it to His own—as a private, then as a more public event. The next stage in the expression of the apprehension of the unique person of the Lord is the placing of the consecrating of His human nature at conception; whereas for Paul He is the self-humbling heavenly Son, yet to the deep thinker of the Fourth Gospel even this interpretation is inadequate for the Greek world now entering on the Church's heritage, the earthly Lord is the Incarnation of the Eternal divine Word.]

It seems quite reasonable that the startling and apparently unexpected testing of the Messiah (which John omits), the account of which must go back in the last resort to a self-communication of the Master to the disciples, should be attributed to the Holy Spirit's guidance as part of the divine plan; though we can hardly ascribe the setting as it stands to Jesus, but to primitive Christian reflexion on the event, (a) iii., and the part taken by the

Spirit is more prominent in L. We should be mistaken if we were to lay too much stress on the claim made indirectly in the synagogue at Nazareth at the outset of the Ministry (according to Luke, (a) v.), as there is evidence of a purposeful artistic transposition of the episode, and such a claim at that time is not in accord with the silence otherwise observed by our Lord in the early months of His Ministry. Similarly the remark concerning Jesus' inspired joy, introducing matter common to M. and L., is peculiar to L., (a) vi. There is only one instance of our Lord's referring to the Holy Spirit as empowering Him in His acts of mercy (M. xii. 28), but here the parallel in L. (xi. 20 ἐν δακτύλῳ θεοῦ) may be preferable, as claiming God's power, though without mention of the Spirit, and the turn of phrase, if anthropomorphic, is more Jewish.

This reference occurs in connexion with that very difficult passage common to all the Synoptists (Mk iii. 29, M. xii. 31 f., L. xii. 10), which gives us varying forms (not indeed strictly parallel) of the saying or sayings of Jesus concerning blasphemy against the Holy Spirit, as operating in and through His beneficent acts; their own successful exorcisms they would not think of attributing to demonic agency, why then should His foes be so blind as to infer the help of Beelzebul in His case? the warped judgement was their own fault, it was the sin of spiritual obtuseness. Even in this instance, therefore, the claim to the Spirit upon Him is indirectly made, Jesus' power is divine in origin, His works of love are ultimately God's works; the functions of the Spirit and of the Messiah are intimately associated.

There remain those verses with regard to the future of the Kingdom after the close of the incarnate life which allude to the Holy Spirit; they are in two passages only, the one, (*b*) ii., is due to the interpretation from Christian life (L. xi. 13),—surely the 'good things' from the Father in answer to prayer (M. vii. 11) meant that Holy Spirit of the Church's vivid realization : the other apparently reflects the story of early persecution at the hands of the Jews and others ('rulers and kings'), in which the form of defence as witnesses to Christ on the part of the disciples is ascribed to the teaching of the Holy Spirit (*b*) iii., Mk xiii. 11, M. x. 20. If the former be patient of the interpretation of a more ethical and continuous experience (leading towards Johannine thought), the latter is surely special and occasional in its application, but at any rate the Spirit's activity succeeds in time (as regards the Church) that of the incarnate Lord; it may be that the present form of the tradition hardly represents the original words of Jesus. When we combine this last with the reference in L. (xxi. 15) to the apology of the disciples in time to come, the 'I will give you a mouth and wisdom' seems to prepare the way for that ambiguity of treatment that we have in our Fourth Gospel concerning the sending of the Spirit from the Father or the glorified Jesus (cf. Ac. ii. 33, xvi. 7), and the Pauline interchange of Spirit of Jesus or of Christ or of God; while, possibly, a combination of the two modes of expression may be discovered in Apoc. xix. 10, 'the witness of Jesus is the Spirit of prophecy.' This forward view is not different in kind from the one allusion of Jesus to the Spirit as inspiring the Biblical writers (Mk xii. 36 = M. xxii. 43), quoting from Ps. cx., quite in the manner of Apostolic references in Ac.

We find then in the teaching and conversations of our Lord, as reported by the Synoptists, no direct assertion that is well established claiming the Holy Spirit as the inspirer of His message and work. There must be some reason for this silence. It can hardly be due to the silence of the narrators, for they are willing (esp. L.) to attribute freely the activity of the Spirit in persons and events. It seems to be the silence of the Master. And if we ask the why and the wherefore of it, we shrink from the attempt to probe the consciousness of Jesus, so far from the event, and with so brief an account of His sayings and discourses. Yet the most reverent criticism must seek some cause. May it be that the immediacy of His communion with the Father was such that He did not need to speak of His endowment with the Messianic Spirit, and that in His training of the Twelve He led them to treasure a direct access to the Father in prayer during the days of His flesh? Hints we possess, indeed, of allusions to the Holy Spirit when His bodily presence was to be removed, as teaching and inspiring the disciples in days of coming stress, as their unseen Pleader before men; in some such converse briefly reported, we find the link which binds events in the Acts and discourses in the Fourth Gospel to the teaching of our Lord Himself. The Holy Spirit would inspire His followers according to their need for the continuing of His work among men.

No mention has been made of that portion of the 'great command' contained in M. xxviii. 19. We do not desire to enter the arena of controversy on the subject; suffice it to say that not only are the words attributed to the risen Lord rather as a summary of the aim of His Church's life, than as prescribing a formula, but there seems little doubt that as men were baptized by the disciples during the Ministry (cf. J. iv. 2) possibly with some such formula as the 'name of Jesus' (cf. frequent occurrence of ἐν τῷ ὀνόματί μου, and the easting out of devils in His name, L. ix. 49), so the original formula after Pentecost would most probably be 'in' or 'into the name of Jesus'; for 'in my name,' which accords with this supposition, as also does the evidence in the book of the Acts, is just that expression which possibly has been the original reading in this verse, seeing that it occurs so frequently in Eusebius, with his access to MSS. now lost, and, but for the Didache, in no writer till Irenæus is the full and exact Matthæan form extant. For cogent arguments against this, cf. J. T. S. VI. 481 ff.

The Church saw rightly the fulfilling of the aim of her Founder in her act of baptizing men, in penitent and believing self-consecration, into a fellowship that was divine, in the glory and joy of the threefold revelation which she had experienced.

§ 2. ACTS.

We are compelled to give some separate treatment to Luke's second volume, despite the similarity sometimes of language and phrase with the references in his Gospel. And for this reason : no one can read the vivid and intense pages of the early chapters of the Acts without feeling that even the written record betrays a consciousness of unmeasured power, a heroic enthusiasm in the face of man and circumstance, an overmastering realization of divine guidance swaying the leaders and the communities in ways unexpected and before unexperienced. Sources and editor alike agree in making the Feast of Pentecost the day of transformation, the birthday of the Church's life; and the phenomena then manifested for the first time are of such frequent recurrence in the early experience of the communities that their manifestation was, for some period at least, recognized as the chief attestation of the presence or gift of the Spirit of God. The humanly unaccountable 'speaking with tongues' was so abnormal, so strange, yet so potent a religious factor that it could not but be divine in origin, a gift from God mediated by the Spirit.

The whole book glows in the light of this primary fact, and back to it all the activities of the Church as witness to Jews and Gentiles for salvation in the name of the risen Lord are traced. It might be termed 'The Acts of the Holy Spirit' in and through Peter, Paul, and other leaders.

At the outset of the book, the Holy Spirit is regarded as the medium of the glorified Lord's revelation to His own for the work of witness (i. 2, 8); and the 'power from on high' (L. xxiv. 49), the gift outpoured at Pentecost, was Christ's to promise and to bestow (ii. 33). The disciples, like their Master, according to the Gospels, were to receive baptism themselves in or with the Holy Spirit (i. 5), and Peter tells how he recalled this in the house of Cornelius, when the 'falling' of the Holy Spirit upon Gentiles was made manifest (xi. 17, 16). Again, in the address on the same occasion, Peter refers to the Baptism of Jesus as an anointing by God 'with the Holy Spirit and with power' (x. 38). If we include the allusion to the 'Spirit of Jesus' (xvi. 7) which may imply a special vision determining the Apostolic plan, these are the only passages which give us direct information as to how the Spirit was regarded to be related to Jesus: the Spirit takes the place of the incarnate Lord. But the time for metaphysical differentiation was not yet, it would

be unreasonable to try to deduce any clear-cut doctrine
concerning 'personal' distinctions, seeing that for the
immediate purpose of a revelation of the divine will to
a Christian leader the compiler did not deem it necessary
to describe the nature of its source in fixed terms: e.g., in
the last reference, it is the Holy Spirit (xvi. 6) that
hinders, then the Spirit of Jesus (7), finally, God who
calls in the vision at Troas (10); it is sufficient that the
revelation is recognized as denoting God's will, though
the expressions used to describe it may vary.

In Luke's Gospel there is an apparently disconnected
promise of the Spirit's assistance given by Jesus to the
disciples, for times of defence before human courts: 'the
Holy Spirit shall teach you...what ye ought to say' (xii.
12); and this promise of future help through the Spirit
might serve as the theme for many passages in the Acts.
To the Spirit is attributed the guidance   (1) of the
Church in assembly. He 'speaks' by some member (xiii.
2), and 'sends forth' Barnabas and Saul (xiii. 4). He is
regarded as the author of the conciliar epistle (xv. 28),
and chooses the ἐπίσκοποι of Ephesus (xx. 28);
(2) of the Apostles and others: Stephen (vi. 10), Philip
(viii. 29, 39), Peter (x. 19, xi. 12). In such connexions
the Spirit is treated as the continuer of the work of the
Messiah, and thus is associated in idea with the theme of
John xiv.; indeed, παράκλησις of the infant community
is ascribed to the Holy Spirit (ix. 31).

At the same time, less personal phrases are very frequently used. The Spirit was in some sense God in action,
and yet a power, a gift from Him.   (a) Filling—
Apostles with the extraordinary manifestations of glossolaly (ii. 4), Peter (iv. 8), all those assembled at prayer
(iv. 31), the Seven (vi. 3), especially Stephen (vi. 5, vii. 55

vision), Saul (ix. 17), Barnabas (xi. 24), Paul (xiii. 9), 'disciples' (xiii. 52).

(*b*) Given—by God, to penitent Jews (ii. 38), to the obedient (v. 32), to Gentiles (xv. 8). Cf. viii. 18, 20.

(*c*) Outpoured—on disciples (ii. 33), on Gentiles (x. 45).

(*d*) Falling—recognized by special phenomena (viii. 16, x. 44, xi. 15).

(*e*) Received—viii. 15, 17, 19 (after imposition of hands), also probably with effect of 'tongues' by which the 'coming' was manifest (xix. 6, also after imposition).

Thus personal and impersonal language alike is used with no sense of inconsistency, the bestower and the bestowed are both God's, and both 'holy.'

We cannot expect to be able to harmonize the modes of narration of the diverse sources from which Luke derived his Palestinian stories; yet we cannot help noting that it is in the earlier portion of the book, just as in the Gospel of the Infancy in the 'former treatise,' that the use of the term Holy Spirit is dominant, about three times the number of instances in cc. xiii.—xxviii.

There is an hypostatizing in the Ananias story; the lie, Peter is reported to have said, is to the Holy Spirit (v. 3), to the Spirit of the Lord (9), to God (4), only varied expressions with the same inner meaning, the divine Spirit working through the instrument, the Apostle; forcibly reminding us of the wilful 'lie in the soul' (M. xii. 32 ‖), so also God's will is 'resisted' through the rejection of the Apostolic (Stephen's) preaching (vii. 51).

But the same Spirit 'spake unto the fathers,' He was the medium of inspiration of the Scriptures, so of David's words (i. 16, iv. 25); thus obvious misunderstanding of the sacred writing is a sin against Him (vii. 51 above); Paul, too, is represented in the concluding address to the Jews at Rome as ascribing words from the book of Isaiah that were put into the mouth of Jahweh to the Holy Spirit (xxviii. 25).

Nor had this inspiration which was attributed to the prophets of old ceased for ever; the periods barren of prophecy were passed away, the consciousness of a daily working of the Spirit in their midst was overwhelmingly real to the disciples, and there were many fit vehicles of His to speak in His name when occasion demanded, whether in the more general sense of prophesying, or in the narrower one of foretelling; He was the medium of prophetic revelation now, He used men for reasonable utterance as well as for the incoherent and uncontrolled manifestation of 'tongues' (cf. 1 Cor. xiv.): e.g., the prophet in xi. 28, speakers in various places (xx. 23) warning Paul not to go up to Jerusalem (xxi. 4), as Agabus did in a still more vivid manner (xxi. 11).

Perhaps it is another small item in favour of $\pi\upsilon\rho\acute{\iota}$ in the original form of M. iii. 11 ‖, that the disciples of the Baptist (xix. 2) knew nothing of Messiah's baptizing $\dot{\epsilon}\nu$ $\pi\nu\epsilon\acute{\upsilon}\mu\alpha\tau\iota$ $\dot{\alpha}\gamma\acute{\iota}\varphi$, in contrast to that of water $\epsilon\acute{\iota}\varsigma$ $\mu\epsilon\tau\acute{\alpha}\nu\omicron\iota\alpha\nu$.

Varied, then, though the material may be, and diverse in historical value, which Luke has worked into his second volume, especially in the stories of Aramaic colouring that the opening chapters contain (and with which the Birth narratives in the Gospel bear comparison), the general unity of style is coupled with a unity of plan, an artistic yet apologetic scheme, which continued study of the Acts only serves to make more clear; and the plan is so far Pauline in that it traces the offering of the good-news of salvation in Christ first to the Jews, who increasingly reject it, then to the Gentiles, whose acceptance thereof grows and spreads continually, and this is in accord with the prefatory words of the author. Further, the development of Christianity outwards from Jerusalem to Rome is by implication put into words of the ascending Master in the opening verses (Ac. i. 8). Luke dedicates his work to one to whom the faith is commended as something acceptable to the Roman world. Thus there is an inevitable foreshortening of the historic perspective. No doubt the doctrine of the Spirit working in and through Messiah and specially chosen instruments of the divine Will was a Jewish inheritance, no doubt the abnormal and surprising phenomena in the early Judæan community were attributed to His influence; nevertheless the fact remains that it is in Luke's work alone that the efficient cause of the various stages of the Church's growth is so frequently and regularly identified with the Holy Spirit.

And this treatment, we have seen in the previous section, affects the preparation for the earthly ministry as well as the succeeding spread of the Christian congregations; so that even in the Gospel, Luke uses πνεῦμα ἅγιον 13 times to the 9 of Mk and M. together, while the term is used in some form no less than 41 times in Acts alone.

The Holy Spirit then is a great reality in Luke's thought-world, it dominates his conceptions. He is the divine guiding power in the Church's growth throughout, though it is indefinite whether the Father or Jesus (i. 4, ii. 33) 'sends' Him, or whether He is a Person or a Power; and for this reason apparently the modes of speech vary, because the conceptions are still fluid, and they are so because they simply describe a living experience, because the author has a vivid realization of the work of the Holy Spirit in Christian life around him, in the congregations perhaps to a large extent Pauline. And yet the truly Pauline level of teaching is unattained, the doctrine of the Spirit as the moulder and fashioner of the Christian's inner life continually, as it confronts us in the Apostle's letters, is unassimilated. Thus Luke, after all, reflects a less developed form of teaching in his writings than his greater fellow-traveller; he edits his sources in the light of the Spirit's work, but that work is still to him almost solely confined to the equipment of the Messiah, of those who prepare His way, and of those who lead on the continuation of His saving mission. The guidance is occasional, mostly external or by 'tongues' and 'prophecy,' the daily religion of the believer is not yet by Luke expressly regarded as the sphere of the influence of the Spirit of God or of Christ.

§ 3. HEBREWS AND CATHOLIC EPISTLES.

It is with some initial surprise that we discover how little trace there is in Hebrews or the so-called Catholic Epistles (apart from 1 John) of any very well defined teaching concerning the Spirit in the use of the term on the divine side.

The contrast as we approach them from the compilations of Luke or the letters of Paul is very great; and yet it is probable that each author knew something of the Pauline correspondence (Jude, 1 Peter, 2 Peter), teaching (Heb.), or at least influence (Ja.).

Only a dozen references to the divine Spirit at the most occur. There is no direct mention of any relation between the Spirit and Jesus, or the early leaders of the Christian communities.

Hebrews. The author of the Hebrews regards the

Holy Spirit quite in the primitive and Jewish manner as the medium of O.T. revelation, quoting a Psalm with the formula 'as saith the Holy Spirit' (iii. 7), and Jeremiah as 'the Holy Spirit witnesseth' (x. 15); while the opening verse of the Epistle says 'God spake to the fathers in or by the prophets.' And not only so, but the ritual regulations of old were ordained of the Holy Spirit for purposes of teaching (ix. 8).

However, the writer fully recognizes a similar inspiration in his contemporaries, who as Christians became sharers at baptism of the Holy Spirit (vi. 4), and this is called in the previous clause 'the heavenly gift,' which reminds us of the second Petrine address at Jerusalem (Ac. ii. 38, cf. ii. 2). This endowment, nevertheless, is variable in effect according to the capacities of men, there are 'dividings' of the Holy Spirit according to God's will (ii. 4), and this is in line with the teaching of Paul (1 Cor. xii.). Here an inclination might be detected towards a more constant influence of the Spirit in daily life, but the previous clause relates rather to special and occasional manifestations of power. Thus Hebrews cannot be safely appealed to for more than this, that the Spirit is imparted to Christians at baptism, and that He, or God, is regarded as speaking through the sacred writings of old.

James. If James be an early work, as the title claims, the absence of any allusion to the Holy Spirit is striking in view of the Lucan interpretation of early events in Palestine. But if, in the difficult passage (iv. 5), it is the divine Spirit to whom the jealous longing is to be attributed, that is the only possible reference to the Spirit, without as well as within man, in the Epistle. There is then an ethical turn in the longing of the Spirit of God for the human soul, akin to the ruling idea in the parable of the Lost Son, and similar to the personal activity ascribed to the indwelling Spirit in Paul. Cf. Ro. xv. 30.

1 Peter. While Hebrews mentions the Holy Spirit (unlike O.T. usage) as 'speaking' through the old prophets, 1 Peter goes further in relating that Spirit to the pre-existent Christ, 'the Spirit of Christ in them,' the prophets (i. 11), even so should it be a gen. of apposition (cf. 2 Cor. iii. 17), the Spirit which is Christ. Somewhat similarly words from the scriptures are used in Heb. (ii. 11 f.) as if Christ spoke them, and Paul represents Christ as the spiritual rock of Rabbinic story. Revelation, therefore, is regarded as essentially divine in origin, whether actually ascribed to God, the Spirit, or Christ.

There is also in this Epistle an allusion looking back to the previous generation of Christians, those who evan-gelized the readers 'in the Holy Spirit sent from heaven' (i. 12, cf. Heb. vi. 4). Here again we have the endowment for missionary witness familiar in Ac. (cf. J. xiv. 26, L. xii. 12, xxiv. 49), sent at Pentecost.

The Spirit too is the agent or instrument of sanc-tification, according to the title of the Epistle, where a personal interpretation is further suggested by the collocation 'foreknowledge of the Father...in sanctification of (or by) the Spirit...the blood of Jesus Christ' (i. 2). This use, coupled with the Isaianic phrase concerning 'the Spirit of glory and of God' resting on the per-secuted saints (iv. 14), forms the nearest approach to the doctrine of the Spirit as an abiding inward personal possession.

There remain the difficult verses in Jude and 2 Peter, the interpretation of which is insufficiently certain to make any reliable addition to the doctrine afforded by the few references in these Epistles and Hebrews.

Jude. Very possibly the first allusion in Jude (19) is to dangerous people who draw distinctions or cause divisions among Christians, boasting themselves to be 'spiritual' yet πνεῦμα μὴ ἔχοντες in the writer's judgement, presumably when tested according to their conduct, considered to have become unworthy of the Spirit from God, once bestowed (?); but the actual allusion remains obscure to us.

The following verse (20), however, demands that the reference should be to the Spirit from God as affecting the inward man, for the worthy behaviour of the true 'πνευματικοί' is 'praying in or by the Holy Spirit.' This is in agreement with the Pauline test of the Spirit's guidance being the life of the individual Christian. The phrase here, it is noteworthy, forms part of another triple coordination of terms, ἐν πνεύματι ἁγίῳ...ἐν ἀγάπῃ θεοῦ ...τὸ ἔλεος τοῦ κυρίου 'I. X.

2 Peter. This passage is not worked directly into 2 Peter, but in the only πνεῦμα reference the authors of the sacred writings are spoken of in the later Jewish manner as 'driven' or 'borne along' by the powerful breath of God (i. 21): it is probably the last in time and the strongest figure of inspiration contained in the N.T.

§ 4. PAUL.

When we pass over to the letters of Paul, so rich do we find them in references to the Holy Spirit, so numerous are the allusions to the Spirit of or from God in the life of the Christian, that it is well to group some, without setting down again all, of the passages, in order to perceive the trend of the evidence.

1. We take first a few of what we may call the Personal references, where activities are predicated of the Spirit that we should consider to mark distinctly personal life of thought and will and act: the Spirit, that is, is conceived as external to man.

The Spirit leads men Gal. v. 18, Ro. viii. 14, has the fruit of His operation in a man's character Gal. v. 22, sanctifies and so prepares for the acceptance of truth 2 Th. ii. 13; witnesses with our spirit Ro. viii. 16, helps and intercedes for us viii. 26, (perhaps) loves xv. 30; searches the deep things of God 1 Cor. ii. 10, cf. 11, 14, works all the varied manifestations xii. 7 ff., (probably) affording fellowship 2 Cor. xiii. 13; also in Eph., which shews an extension of Pauline teaching, revealing iii. 5, source of unity iv. 3 f., capable of being grieved iv. 30.

2. Again, we can contrast some of the allusions which imply rather the influence, gift, or power effected in man, where we might almost use for equivalents terms such as the new man, new nature, new creation; and, because the emphasis is rather on the sphere of action within the Christian, we could differentiate by means of small letters. Here the standpoint is that of the recipient and user of the power in him that is ascribed to the Person.

On the one hand this is a gift, 1 Th. iv. 8, Ro. v. 5, Gal. iii. 5, cf. Phil. i. 19, 2 Cor. i. 22; on the other it is regarded as received, Gal. iii. 2, 14, Ro. viii. 15, 1 Cor. vi. 19, vii. 40, 2 Cor. xi. 4.

3. Further, we can give a few examples of what might be named an inclusive usage, seeing that it is possible to think of the divine and human aspects together, the source and the effect, or separately; and for us the actual mind of the writer at the moment cannot be certainly determined.

The Spirit is sent into our hearts Gal. iv. 6, by the Spirit we walk (v. 16) and live (25), where it may be the human spirit as it is affected by the divine Spirit. So in the 'indwelling' passages, we may think of the Person or His influence within, or both, for the unseen power within is God's—or Christ's—representative. Ro. viii. 9, 11, 1 Cor. iii. 16, 2 Ti. i. 14, cf. Phil. iii. 3.

Again, we can classify references according as the results are (a) external, special, occasional, or (b) internal, normal, continual.

(a) Gal. iii. 2, 5, 1 Th. v. 19, 2 Th. ii. 2, 1 Cor. xii.—xiv. tongues, prophecy, etc.; Ro. xv. 19, 1 Cor. ii. 4 allied with δύναμις; Eph. iii. 5, vi. 18, 1 Ti. iv. 1 seem also of the charismatic type.

(b) In our hearts Gal. iv. 6, Ro. viii. 9, 16, producing within joy Ro. xiv. 17, 1 Th. i. 5, hope Ro. xv. 13, love Ro. v. 5, liberty 2 Cor. iii. 17, sanctification 2 Th. ii. 13, 1 Cor. vi. 11, Ro. xv. 16, strength Eph. iii. 16, renewal Tit. iii. 5, generally effective in character Gal. v. 22, 2 Cor. vi. 6. To such as these all allusions to indwelling may be added, and such as imply a present possession within, 1 Cor. ii. 10 ff., 2 Cor. i. 22, v. 5, etc. These few references are sufficient to demonstrate the dominance of the double idea of inwardness and continuance. There are indeed many ways in which we can rearrange the data provided by the Pauline passages, but the gain in detail would not add much for the purpose of grasping the outstanding features of the Apostle's teaching. This doctrine concerning the Holy Spirit, whether viewed primarily according to the context as the Person exercising the influence or the influence exercised, must not be regarded as something entirely new: there must have been some preparatory sympathy in hearers or readers, teaching totally fresh would have raised some discussion. There was evidently no cleavage as in the case of the controversy about legal ordinances; indeed, to make it intelligible, views and ideas familiar to Christians generally, and known among those to whom the Apostle wrote, must be presupposed.

There would be the Jewish inheritance common to himself and his compatriots in various quarters, there would be the Tarsian birth and education to put him in touch with Hellenic and Asian conceptions of inspiration, there would be also the daily experiences and thoughts of the Jewish churches of Palestine, which perforce reacted upon him when he came into their midst, perhaps even when he was their persecutor : but last and chiefest of all, there would be the vivid reality of his own personal experience, the vision of the glorified Jesus on the Damascus road.

None of these factors may be omitted from the material of the thought-world of his eager vigorous mind. The opinions and convictions of others of many types, races, and stations in his unremitting intercourse with men must have tended in some measure at least to mould both his reflexion and his expression. As far as we can gather from the records that we possess, it was the sudden, the abnormal, the inexplicable, that fixed the attention of the early congregations, first Jewish, then Gentile at least in part.

To the Israelite, of divine agencies, of unseen powers to which wonders and mysteries unheard of before could be ascribed, there was but one that was expected to mark the days of Messiah, the outpouring of the (Holy) Spirit ; and to this hypostatized divine activity were due all the varied manifestations for which no human explication was available.

Apparently the most common in the early days of the Church, and the manifestation most prized and desired at Corinth and probably elsewhere, was that of 'speaking with tongues.' Paul, too, shared the ecstasy uncontrolled by reason in moments of deep emotion and expectation in the assembly, nor was he without his visions and revelations (1 Cor. xiv. 18, 2 Cor. xii. 1); but he realized the risks and the jealousy which such rendered possible in highly excitable congregations, and when he set about—whether consciously or no—a revaluation of 'spiritual gifts' (1 Cor. xii.—xiv.) there would be, no doubt, others also similarly anxious, and ready to assist in the establishing and maintaining of an orderliness worthy of Christian assemblies. Paul's reflective thought upon 'spiritual' phenomena appears to have led him to take what we may term—to choose a single word—the 'pragmatic' view of the subject. There was a real danger of ecstatic manifestations becoming valueless in a riot of emotion, whether collective or individual: but the believer's was not to be a self-centred experience, it was to be a service, as even the earliest extant letters testify: there were limitations set by discipline and love, the convert had to live for the benefit of others as well, he had a part in the mission of the Messiah, to bring men to and prepare them for Christ.

So the master-builder of Christian congregations expounds directly or indirectly this principle: gifts ascribed to the divine Spirit are of value just according as they are good or useful for something, in the first instance for the Church of which the 'subject' is a member—πρὸς τὸ συμφέρον 1 Cor. xii. 7, πρὸς οἰκοδομήν xiv. 26; and then in the case of quieter gifts more lasting and continuous in effect, for their virtue-producing or character-forming

power in the individual; in so far as they make for
'walking' in the Spirit, in so far as they lead to the
pattern of Christ. Thus even the homeliest graces come
from Him, and are developed under His benign influence
in ordinary life (Gal. v. 22).

The sphere of the Spirit's activity in human life is thus
vastly extended by Paul; not the special and occasional,
the miraculous and mysterious only, but the continuous
and ordinary, the inward and ethical in each disciple's
development is the Holy Spirit's work. And as Paul
contemplated the wondrous change from the old unregenerate man that he had been conscious of so intensely
himself (Ro. vii.), and had seen again and again in others,
that 'metamorphosis' towards the pattern of the Lord,
the new man, the new creation (Gal. vi. 15, 2 Cor. v. 17),
the new nature; all this, he felt, was God's constant care
through the Holy Spirit, the heavenly Being working on
and in and through the human nature of the baptized.
Not man's spirit only was affected, but the religious life
included the bodily habits and welfare, they too must
share the divine immanence, the indwelling presence of
the Spirit of God (1 Cor. vi. 13, 19, etc.).

Paul's ideal for the believer, amidst all the hindrances
that he found to its fulfilment, seems to have been
sinlessness (cf. 1 John) in spiritual and physical life; a
holy life because of the inward holy power, the work of a
holy because divine Person.

But the Apostle went further. The operation of that
Person need not begin only with some vividly realized
manifestation, or limit His effect to some occasional experience of ecstatic phenomenon or rapt vision; rather did
it commence the Christian's life as such, was the very
source and origin of it. As men went back in thought

over the years, they need not draw the line at occasional uprushes of inexplicable origin, but must regard the normal and comparatively smooth development as due throughout to the same divine Spirit's energy. The Spirit's work is from the beginning, that is usually from baptism, at or after which recognized phenomena generally occurred (Ro. viii. 2, 1 Cor. vi. 11, xii. 13). Under the influence of such teaching the mere wonder would decrease in value, and glossolaly become less prominent as the gift of the Spirit; but the dissemination of this doctrine in the soil of human minds that must have been in some way prepared to receive it was epoch-making for Church order, development, and organization, and also it afforded a unifying principle for Christian character as such. Combined with Paul's fervid religion we find the quality of statesmanship: his whole teaching concerning the Spirit—though drawn from him in his letters only as occasion served, beaten out on the anvil of experience, and therefore by no means systematic, and far from being dogmatically definite—is a very profoundly practical revaluation of current and popular Christian views for the service and the benefit of the churches at large. Order must rule in the congregation and the individual member; the worth of 'seizure' by the Spirit is far lower for profit or edification than the 'walk' in the Spirit, that creation of a new thing in the world, the Christlike character.

Thus did Paul above all others, so far as we know, guide into useful channels the abounding and exuberant spiritual manifestations among his converts. But just as he looked back to the opening of the believer's life, so he looked on into its future, he realized its eternal qualities, they too were from the Spirit. The possession of that Spirit in effect and influence here and now was but the pledge and earnest of life beyond time (2 Cor. i. 22, v. 5), the promise of a fuller and richer future; just as the characteristic of the indwelling is life indeed now (Ro. viii. 2, 2 Cor. iii. 6), continually active and daily realized within.

The nature of the evidence available from letters warns us not to expect definite, systematized and philosophically reasoned instruction. We may not read into phrases marked by intense earnestness and religious power the clear distinctions of later centuries, after long and subtle controversies of Greek-trained thinkers; but something must be said concerning the relation of the Spirit and Christ in Paul's writings.

Although the Holy Spirit was unclaimed by the Jews of the latter days, and unclaimed by John the Baptist, scarcely referred to by Jesus (according to the Synoptists), and even in Apocalyptic literature only ascribed to characters of the distant past; yet the primitive communities accepted the Pentecostal phenomena as indubitable testimony that the Messianic accompaniment was indeed a present reality amongst them, so that we are not greatly surprised to find that with Paul the Spirit marks the new dispensation or new covenant, begun by the incarnate life of the Messiah, Son of God. So frequently do we meet with such a contrast that we might express it thus: as the letter is to the Spirit, so is the law to Christ; and this prepares us for an apparent confusion or at least interchange of Christ and the Spirit, or even an identification in effect (2 Cor. iii. 17).

The Holy Spirit's work is Christ's work—functionally, soteriologically, it is the same: He is 'another,' continuing unseen in hearts the work of the once visible Messiah amongst men.

Hence it is that the Spirit only acts upon men and especially upon believers, for Christ is central to Paul. Christology comes before Pneumatology with him as with the Church theologians in days to come, if only for the reason that the conversion-appearance of the exalted Jesus to himself took the place of the Spirit's acknowledged work in many another.

The circle of the incarnate life on earth is ever being extended, as it were, by wider circles, and this very extension is the Spirit's work; but the function is similarly 'unto salvation,' both Christ and the Spirit are divine, and the work is God's: so from the side of the faithful 'in Christ' and 'in the Spirit' are convertible terms. The believers are one body because of Christ (Ro. xii. 5), yet also because of the Spirit (1 Cor. xii. 13); they are 'in Spirit' because the Spirit 'dwells in' them, but the Spirit is also Christ's (Ro. viii. 9 ff.), and they are 'in Christ' (1 Th. onwards): their life is from Christ (2 Cor. iv. 11, Col. iii. 4), but also from the Spirit (Ro. viii. 2): they are baptized into Christ (Gal. iii. 27), yet in the Spirit of God as well (1 Cor. vi. 11).

Moreover, there are passages in which, from the religious standpoint, 'the Spirit of God,' 'the Spirit of Christ,' 'Christ' are equivalent (Ro. viii. 9 ff.). Or again, in the contrasting of 'ministrations,' the Lord and the Spirit are identified, not essentially but in function and effect (2 Cor. iii. 17 f.), be that effect termed righteousness, life, or glory. Each—God, Christ, Spirit—is called 'life-giving' (Ro. viii. 11, 1 Cor. xv. 22, 2 Cor. iii. 6). The operations of each are regarded as being inclusive rather than exclusive, but the language in no instance is of the nature of a metaphysical definition, but is dependent on the practical thought and special point of sight of the context.

In Paul's letters there is no mention of the Spirit as the special source of the inspiration of the Scriptures, although he discovers Christ or the Spirit of Christ present in the events that they relate; nor does he ever use the term simply for God in manifestation or as defining the nature of the Deity (cf. J. iv. 24). Within the inherited monotheism that is dominant in his writings, he yet makes distinctions and those personal in the true sense: having the hypostatizing of Spirit, Wisdom, Memra in the literature of his people as part of the furnishing of his mind, but with the personal consciousness of personal activities and influences in his life, and that of others, as the chief factor. However these modes of being or functions were experienced by men in time, that remains only relative to man; but the Messiah was to Paul preexistent before incarnation, so also was the Spirit ever within the divine Being, both are spoken of as objective realities, and to both is applied language which we use of personal life.

In the occasional coordinations which Paul makes (1 Cor. xii. 4 ff., 2 Cor. xiii. 13, cf. Ro. viii. 11, 16 f., Eph. i. 17, iv. 4 ff., etc.), we have the doctrine of the Trinity, which took many generations to work out in terms of Greek philosophy, informally and in germ only. For Paul is concerned with the Holy Spirit primarily for practical religion, in and for the operation in man for his salvation, especially therefore within the believer in Christ; seeing that as creative, as active in nature, or in the heroes of Israelitish story, even in Apostolic leaders (unless Paul wrote Eph. iii. 5 as it stands) He is unmentioned. Though it is in the Apostle's letters that we have the fullest teaching relating to the Holy Spirit conceived as a divine Person external to man yet operating within him

and that daily; the fragmentariness and lack of anything
of the nature of a systematic treatment in occasional and
edificatory writing render any adequate summarizing into
clear and thorough-going definitions difficult, if not impossible, without reading into language of intensely practical
religious value meanings dependent on developments of
speculative thought in the Church, associated with the
Christological controversies.

We must be content to find in Paul what is present
personal experience verified and verifiable by others then
and now, description rather than definition in strict terms
of the Holy Spirit's Person and work.   Trinitarian
doctrine, that is, is still only implicit not explicit, embryonic not full grown.   The data of the extant relics of
the post-apostolic age as regards references to the Spirit
confirm by their testimony the judgement that Paul was
far in front of his generation.

The freer rule of the Spirit to which he trusted so
much was necessarily checked by the very growth and
organization of the Christian churches.

§ 5. JOHANNINE WRITINGS.

When we review the passages collected from those
writings to which the name of John is attached, we are
arrested at once by the apparent disharmonies if not con-
tradictions therein.

Gospel. In the Fourth Gospel there is a series of
references in line with the Synoptic narrative, which
make mention of the Spirit's 'descending' on the Son
of God, Who could therefore have the Messianic prero-
gative of baptizing with or in 'holy spirit' (i. 32 f.), but
no record is given of the Baptism of Jesus.   Moreover,

assuming that in iii. 34 the later gloss ὁ θεός marks the correct subject of δίδωσιν, the endowment is upon Him in all its fulness; cf. the dove symbolism in the Synoptists. But the incarnate Logos as Messiah also imparts this gift to His own after His glorification (vii. 39), with which xx. 22 virtually agrees, where the ancient identification of 'spirit' and 'breath' is prominent, as breathing is the symbolic mode of conveying the gift from the risen Christ. If one of these references be secondary, the close of vii. 39 from its variable transmission is the more likely to be so; but that seems hardly needful, when we bear in mind all the experience of the Church starting from the Pentecostal effusion (which the bestowal xx. 22 replaces); for the question in vii. 39 is not of the essential nature of the Spirit, but of the special aspect as indwelling the Messianic adherents after the Lord's departure: the 'living water' symbol links the passage with the thought of iv. 14, which seems also to have reference to the possession of the Spirit by the disciples.

In the conversation with Nicodemus we are struck by what appears to be a somewhat different conception of birth 'from the Spirit' (iii. 5, 6, 8, ἄνωθεν 3, 7), while elsewhere the new birth is 'from God' (i. 13), and entirely so in the Epistle, 9 times. (There is no mention of 'spirit' in 2, 3 John.)

Quite apart from the question of a common authorship of the Gospel and Epistle, the uniqueness and what we may call the Pauline character of these few verses at least incline us to assume the writer to be capable of holding two distinct views without making a real attempt to reconcile or to unify them: if so, the more mystical mode of thought would appear to be that native to himself, and the mediation of the Spirit in the new birth would reflect Christian opinion around him. We seem compelled to seek some such reason if we are to extend that frequent allusiveness in words reported of Jesus (iv. 13 f., vii. 33 f., xii. 32 etc.) to a purposeful ambiguity in treatment of facts of Christian history and experience. Is the 'Spirit' source or 'God,' or are they terms really undifferentiated in the author's mind? It may be possible to find a connecting link in the Samaria episode (iv. 23 f.), where the essential nature of God is said to be πνεῦμα, and therefore acceptable worship must be of a 'spiritual' kind (ἐν πνεύματι καὶ ἀληθείᾳ).

In like manner the utterances of the Logos incarnate, as θεός (i. 1), partake of the nature of 'spirit' (vi. 63), have an inward divine energy ascribed to them; and in this context the cleavage between the realms of 'spirit' and 'flesh' is as marked as in iii. 6 etc.; only the Logos can bestow the life 'from above,' and this is associated closely in the Church's experience with the Spirit-gift at baptism.

But now another antinomy, seemingly in thought as well as form, is manifest; and it is perhaps that which renders some inclined to suspect another hand of the same school, to whom in view of Church traditions the Spirit's work was insufficiently prominent. Be that as it may, on the surface at any rate there is not a uniform treatment as regards the Spirit in the so-called Last Discourses. In c. xiv. the Paraclete or Advocate (16) is hypostatized as a divine Person with the Logos and identified with the Spirit, here named τὸ πνεῦμα τῆς ἀλη-θείας or τὸ ἅγιον (17, 26); but by virtue of His witness, He is ἄλλος, distinct, but not differing therefore in kind from the Word in office and function, and His presence is permanent in the Apostles, the Church as opposed to 'the world.' He is given (16) or sent (26) by the Father to teach and call to mind the content of the Son's revelation when upon earth. But the next occurrence (xv. 26) speaks in a different way of the Paraclete being sent by Jesus, yet παρὰ τοῦ πατρός, and He is further the same as the Spirit of truth ὃ παρὰ τοῦ πατρὸς ἐκπορεύεται, and His office is that of witness concerning (περί) Jesus. Once more, the 'mission' of the Paraclete is by Jesus (xvi. 7), and conditioned by His departure, and the identification with the Spirit of truth follows (13). He 'comes' to 'guide' to a complete knowledge concerning Jesus, as regards the disciples,—and this is a much larger meaning than that in the Synoptic tradition of assistance in personal defence at times of persecution and judicial procedure—but as regards Jesus, to 'glorify' Him through the Church in face of the world. Now these conceptions of the Spirit's mission and work seem reconcilable only by regarding the presence of the Spirit given or sent in His name as equivalent in the mind and language of the writer to the continued presence of Jesus Himself in the believers (cf. xiv. 18, 28). And as to the work of the Spirit, it is only xv. 26, xvi. 14 that His mission is from Jesus, His 'witness' to Jesus, or 'glorification' of Jesus. His presence, and that abiding, may be a view on the line of direct development from the occasional sense in Ac. i. 8, ii. 32 f.; where we may discover a link of connexion, the Spirit is 'received' by the risen Jesus παρὰ τοῦ πατρός (as J. xv. 26), and 'outpoured' with visible effect by Him on His disciples. This is no doctrine of 'procession,' it is the bestowal that is prominent, whether from the Father or Jesus. But whatever be the true solution, if attainable, of these difficulties, they serve as a warning to us not to expect anything in the way of systematized doctrine in occasional writings such as Paul's, or in literature with a purpose, such as the Fourth Gospel (xx. 31); for the Spirit symbolized living experiences in the communities, but the conceptions were fluid still, and only partly harmonized : the age of philosophic reflexion was not yet.

Epistle. The attribution of the term Paraclete to Jesus in 1 J. ii. 1 agrees with J. xiv. 16 (ἄλλον), and serves to mark a distinction in the mode of help. Jesus is Paraclete on behalf of the sinner towards the Father for forgiveness, the Spirit is so on behalf of the Father (or Christ) towards the disciples for witness (truth).

In the Epistle also the Spirit is God's (iii. 24 according to the usual interpretation), and the abiding presence is that of God in the believer from the time of the baptismal gift (aor. iii. 24), and this abiding is continual (pf. iv. 13). Thus θεός can be predicated by inference of the Spirit as well as of the Logos. Again in this Epistle the Spirit's office of witness to the content of faith regarding the incarnate Word is also emphasized (v. 6), behind and greater than any external sacramental testimony (v. 8 ?). Finally, whether any genuine converse had been treasured in the mind of a disciple or not, it seems beyond doubt that the actual realizations of the Church and her hopes for the future, and the struggle against rising speculation of a docetic type forced upon her from within and without, have been reflected in the mode of reporting words of Jesus in regard of the promise of the Paraclete and the related and soon much-debated subject of the Parousia (cf. M. xxviii. 20, 2 P. iii. 4, J. xvi. 16 ff.). The undoubted experience of the Church and of individual believers put the Spirit and the Word as coordinate. Rather than making any open affirmation concerning philosophic distinctions,

their language describes divine activities as personally
known and felt as relating to men ; and the starting-point
of fresh conceptions of God's Being was the historic life
of Jesus.

In some places in the Epistle we are reminded of that
permanent distinction between spirit-life and flesh-life
which the Gospel draws (iii. 6), in the contrast between
the spirits that are ἐκ τοῦ θεοῦ, and those that manifest
themselves in false prophecy and wrong belief (iv. 1 ff.).
Here we seem to come upon a later phase of that prominent difficulty of Church experience as Paul knew it,
how to determine the source of a presumably 'spiritual'
utterance (1 Cor.); but in this case the immediate test of
genuineness—or rather of a divine impulse in the individual concerned—is the confession of a true incarnation as
opposed to holding docetic views under Gnostic influence.
In iv. 1 it is 'the spirits' because of different members
speaking in the congregation, or, maybe, setting themselves
up rather as teachers on the ground of some revelation,
and manifesting the influence of either 'the Spirit of truth'
or 'the spirit of error'; the former expression recalling
v. 7 where the Spirit not only is characterized by truth
but is the Truth, and also the identification of the same
with the Paraclete (J. xiv. 17, xv. 26, xvi. 13), whereas
the latter may have a parallel in Paul's τὸ ψεῦδος 2 Th.
ii. 11.

Nevertheless this doctrinal test is by no means the
only one of the God-given Spirit in the Christian, there
is a test of conduct as well as of religious confession, those
who accept Jesus as Saviour, Son, Messiah, exhibit a life
dominated by love (iv. 13 context). Here again we are
not far from the constructive ethical teaching of Paul
concerning the Spirit.

Apocalypse. Although some cannot believe that the various features of the mission and manifestation of the Holy Spirit in Gospel and Epistle have been filtered through the same mind and have flowed from the same pen, it is incomparably harder to attain to any conviction that the Apocalypse is of the same authorship, albeit that it might reflect earlier phases of Christian thought in the same locality. The treatment of the Spirit is quite different from that in the other Johannine writings. The conditions are those of vision and prophecy. Oriental speculation and Jewish Apocalyptic have been laid under contribution, whether portions of the material have been incorporated, or utilized by the seer's mind as apparatus for his visions.

1. The seven spirits that confront us at once (i. 4, iii. 1, iv. 5, v. 6) lead our thoughts back to planetary beings, star-spirits, ministers of the Lord of hosts whose characteristic, if not substance, is light (cf. i. 12, iv. 5, v. 6), at the service of the glorified Jesus.

2. On the other hand we have messages from 'the Spirit,' that are not distinguished from those of the glorified Lord which precede, Who has the attributes of God (ii. 11 with 8 etc.); but it is hard to say whether the Spirit in such connexion is to be regarded as visualized by the 'prophet,' objectively hypostatized, or as the divine voice speaking within, through the mind of the seer; the latter would perhaps agree better with xiv. 13 and xxii. 17, and in xix. 10 we find that the activity of the Spirit in the Christian prophets has the same function as that of the embodied Jesus (supposing Ἰησοῦ subjective), that is witness; so that in revealing significance their functions are equivalent, and the message is in each case God's (xxii. 6).

3. The seer records his 'becoming in spirit' (i. 10,

iv. 2) on being carried up as Ezekiel of old in his vision, a marked feature in itself of Apocalyptic description (cf. the Temptation narratives). Here we have language quite suitable to Jewish Christian Churches (cf. Ac.), and especially so to Asian communities with a race-consciousness of excitable religion. Primitive and Hebrew relationship is likewise observable in the references to the breath of life (xi. 11, xiii. 15) and to the unclean spirits (xvi. 13, xviii. 2).

It appears to be reasonable to hold that 'the seven spirits' are not the Spirit, but ministerial agencies (cf. Heb. i. 14) at the service of the heavenly Lord; and that between the Spirit and Christ exalted there is as regards influence no clear distinction drawn.

There is a certain amount of common property in language descriptive of the Spirit working in early Christian individuals (prophets) and communities, but the book stands by itself as the only specimen of Apocalyptic compilation within the N.T. writings, and its main purpose is encouragement of the saints in persecution. It cannot be said to make any real contribution to our knowledge of the work of the Holy Spirit, except in so far as He is associated with 'prophecy' in the Church.

§ 6.   THE APOSTOLIC FATHERS.

We do not desire to extend the inquiry further, but from such literature of the next age within the Church as has been preserved to us, we find results that are sufficiently remarkable; results which go to shew that the deepest and most ethical teaching, that which we cherish most now, that contained in Pauline and Johannine writings, is just that which is the least prominent.

Assuredly we must remember that we possess but relics of probably a considerable amount of post-apostolic literature even before 150 A.D., but we should hardly expect the survival to be so small or the range so limited after the fuller usage in Lucan books and Pauline letters. For this reason it is worth while to sum up in the briefest possible way the evidence from the so-called Apostolic Fathers, including Justin's Apology also (the Second Apology does not contain πνεῦμα at all).

1.   The Spirit as a gift, outpoured, received etc. is mentioned in Clement four times (twice coordinating Father and Son), by implication twice in Ignatius, in Barnabas once, in Didache and Justin not at all, but about a dozen times in Hermas.

2.   As the medium of inspiration for the O.T. or O.T. characters.   Five times in Clement, Paul also being once called πνευματικός, and also ascribed to the Christian writer: eight times in Barnabas; once in Didache, in words used as well in Barnabas, but also four times of Christian prophecy (twice false), as also Ignatius on two occasions.   Hermas has the Spirit thus twice in his Apocalyptic imagery concerning prophecy in the Church, once 'the angel of the prophetic Spirit,' cf. Asc. Isa. Justin, on the other hand, speaks over twenty times of the 'prophetic Spirit' of God of old, thrice in addition with the attribute 'holy.'

3.   Father, Son and Spirit are named in succession once in Clement, in Didache twice (baptismal formula), thrice in Ignatius (Spirit compared to a rope for the ascent of prayer, and twice in the order Son—Father—Spirit).   The coordination also appears in Justin in baptismal and eucharistic forms, twice each.

4.   The Holy Spirit is associated with the (mode of)

Incarnation once by Ignatius, and nine times by Hermas (all in one passage, Sim. v. vi. 5—7, of the control in the incarnate life rather than of the conception).

5. The divinity of the Spirit comes to prominence only in Hermas, about seven times; while Justin associates the Spirit and the Logos in Creation four times, and once even identifies the Spirit with the Word (twice with 'the power'). Hermas, too, on one occasion seems to make the Son and the Spirit equivalent, and also figuratively identifies the Son and the personified Church.

6. Most remarkable perhaps of all, there seems to be no allusion to the inward operation of the Holy Spirit, unless we reckon Barnabas' references to a 'spiritual temple' as such, except in Hermas, where it is the dominant aspect. In his type of work we might indeed expect it to be so, but hardly to be thus lacking in other authors.

He refers to the (Holy) Spirit as an indwelling presence, a divine representative within man, about nine times; and in quite as many other places does he imply that indwelling with ethical effect in the life.

Thus, as in the N.T., there is no reference except to operation in men, Jews or Christians; but, unlike the N.T., no 'charismata' are named, no 'speaking with tongues' is mentioned even in Hermas, nothing of the primitive extraordinary and unforeseen.

Again, like the N.T., words from the old scriptures are virtually regarded as words of God (Clement, Barnabas, Justin); while, unlike the N.T., the Spirit is not mentioned in direct connexion with the work of witness or of sanctification.

There is no trace of the familiar Pauline operation continually within except in Hermas, and there seems

to be no vestige at all of the specially Johannine conceptions, except in Justin.

Generally speaking, Pauline influence is recognizable
in respect of Spirit teaching only slightly in Clement,
and strongly in Hermas; just those of the writers from
whom we have documents surviving in whom we might
expect to find it, seeing that both are directly connected
with Rome. Paul had not yet come to his own—in regard
of his doctrine concerning the Spirit—in the great Church;
indeed, in some ways he is only doing so to-day.

We find, then, little if any extension of the teachings
which the N.T. writings afford: there is nothing that goes
really further to assist us in defining the nature of the
Holy Spirit or His work; the latter is regarded as mainly
historic, as with Justin, or experimental, as with Hermas.

In these early days there was as yet no necessity to
define belief in the Holy Spirit in a set form of words,
His living presence was realized, His divine influence was
working in the midst of the faithful continually.

The very fact that the conceptions are yet fluid and
the expressions informal tells us that we have still to do
with the sphere of living faith and devotion, and that the
colder age of reflexion and defensive reasoning has not
arrived.

§ 7. PRESENT SIGNIFICANCE.

We have now completed our survey of the early amor-
phous stages of Christian Pneumatology. Starting as we
did from the scanty allusions attributed to Jesus in the
Synoptic Gospels, such as the conversation concerning
the unpardonable sin, that of resolutely turning from an
illuminating manifestation of God's Spirit, where that
Holy Spirit is conceived as 'other' than Jesus, and other

than the Father; or that promise of the Spirit's witness
and help in days of crisis; we discover that the teaching
gains in volume and rises in far-reaching significance for
the individual and the community, as we attain to the
rich and deep conceptions of a Paul and a John.   And
then, amid the early struggles against Christological
heresy, the doctrine of the Holy Spirit is found to fall
into the background in such relics as we possess of the
literature, and Hermas alone appears to carry on, mingled
with much that is of less value, the more inward teaching
of Paul.

But it is no aim of ours now to follow out the gradual
upbuilding of reasoned dogma on the subject of the Person
and work of the Spirit; we have but added to our compendium of all the references in the N.T. in which the
word 'spirit' occurs—the interpretation of many of which
is so hard to determine with exactness—an endeavour to
appreciate the general trend of the teaching therein contained concerning the divine Spirit; profoundly convinced
that the primitive views however flexible in expression
have their contribution to make towards the supplying
of the needs and the fulfilling of the aspirations of men
to-day.

In our teaching of others, especially the young, we
must be to some extent anthropomorphic, seeing that
we can only use terms of human language, and that in
the light of the Incarnation, in our doctrine of God.

Our popular modern notion of 'person'—as signifying
a separate individual (human) being—is totally different
from what 'person' meant or really means when applied
theologically to distinctions within the divine Being.

To those who bow before the mystery of God, and
are humbled in face of the vastness of His operations as

perceived in that corner of creation known but partially to us, and recognize the wonder of His ways in the souls of His children, yet tremble to speak feeble human words of these things, the popular presentation of the doctrine of the Trinity often approaches tritheism, or at the least exceeds the reserve of the N.T.

If mere human words have indeed to be used, as a Hilary or an Augustine felt in later days, defensively, as it were, to express divine mysteries and religious experiences, the externally available material for a reasoned faith in the Holy Spirit lies primarily in the data that we have investigated.

The evidence from the N.T. (Ac. and Paul perhaps especially) teaches us that we must keep in view both aspects of divine-human relationship, the influence and the Person, the Giver and the gift, the spirit and the Spirit; we are conscious, as was the first age of Christians, of the work then of the Worker, of the in-ourselves previous to the Not-in-ourselves. In putting the Person foremost in some instances are we not apt to make or imply distinctions that are too evidently those that we make concerning separate human beings of our experience, and thus are less wise than the N.T. writers, who never attempt to describe the mutually inclusive relations within the divine Being, unless it be in words ascribed to our Lord (e.g. M. xi. 27, xxviii. 18; J. iii. 35)?

The indwelling or inworking of God the Holy Spirit in us is and can only be spiritual, mystical: with none of us is that inworking or indwelling, the divine-human interacting, completely realized—only once historically was it so, in the life of the Incarnate—so that our language describing it can only do it very imperfectly at best.

Confining ourselves to N.T. data, the Spirit is the

Spirit of Jesus, because by Him the Christ is interpreted
to us and in us; yet the Spirit is the Spirit of the Father,
because through the Christ-life comes our revelation in
man of God. As a Person, as $\theta\epsilon\acute{o}s$, as an eternal mode of
the divine Essence, He is separable to thought—ideally—
though we tend to go too far in attempting by our words
to delimit the sphere of His operation, because it transcends our experience. In the words reported of our
Lord, the Spirit is spoken of as separable from the Father,
yet also from Jesus Himself: in the language of a Paul
He is not the Christian whom He helps, nor the Father
to Whom He expresses, as it were, the believer's unformed
petition: to a John He is $\check{a}\lambda\lambda os$, $\dot{\epsilon}\kappa\epsilon\hat{\imath}\nu os$ etc., not the Father,
and not the Word, yet—speaking for human understanding
—He is sent by the Father, or, with the double aspect
of bestowal, by the Son also.

We have also to bear in mind that for well-nigh two
centuries of the Church's life neither the word 'person'
nor the word 'Trinity' was used; still the same experiences were theirs, and if they found other means of
describing them than did later theologians, we may not
therefore call the Christians of those early days un-
orthodox.

But Personality is the loftiest thing that we know,
we recognize it as persisting through physical changes, we
feel compelled to use personal terms in our language concerning the mystery of God: nor can we find a better
word than Person, so long as we take care to remember
that our human ultra-distinctions, the separateness of
individual men, may not be thought of when we are
mentally regarding personal separableness in the essentially inseparable Being of God; guarding against rashness
by reminding ourselves that the N.T. neither speaks of

Three Persons, nor Three, nor Persons, as we do. It is our imperfect effort to make intelligible the threefoldness of God as revealed therein, although neither Paul nor John actually says that the Father, the Son or Logos, and the Spirit are One, or that there are Three in One, because God's inward nature is nowhere defined.

The Personality of the Holy Spirit, separable for human thought, is, as it were, in the background within the N.T., and long remained so, and for this reason : because it is that fact of human history and experience, which we call the Incarnation, that colours all the language, and affects all the terms that we use to describe the relations of God to man. So much is this so, that we discover that the Spirit is only spoken of as related to man—primarily the Christian—individually, and thus to the aggregate, the Church.

The Spirit's relation to the Cosmos has ceased to be mentioned; man is primary. The soteriological point of sight, because of the Incarnation, is supreme.

We realize now, perhaps much more than any Apostles or Apostolic men, how inexpressibly the πρὸς τὸν θεόν relations of the 'Persons' transcend our experience and baffle our most reverent phrasing : because in view of our larger knowledge to-day we must cling above all things to the Unity of God. The Persons are essentially inseparable; yet in functioning, Son and Spirit are identifiable, as with Paul, and, as with John, each is not ἕτερος to the other; from the standpoint of salvation each is doing the same work of God, differently regarded. God is once for all, according to the N.T., realized in humanity by the Son, and in each believer and in the Church as a whole (esp. Eph., Jo.) by the Spirit. In other words, it is through the economy of Redemption that we first realize the Threefoldness.

The doctrine of the Undivided Trinity is built up fundamentally for the Christian from the experimental facts of the revelation in the historic life of Jesus, and the verification of experience is as open to all now as in the first age of vivid faith.　　The one divine Essence is represented to us as shared by the heavenly beings Christ (Logos, Son) and the Spirit, and to each are attributed qualities of thought, will and action which we men can only designate as 'personal'; although to ourselves even human personality is something invisible and intangible, that can only be described in terms of the environment by which it is conditioned; we only know it relatively, and it defies our words to define, how much more so divine personality.

According to Paul and John especially, the Son or Logos and the Spirit are regarded as modes of the divine Being, eternal, within the Godhead; pre-existent that is πρὸς τὸν θεόν, as John says of the Logos, but only known to man relatively, and that in the revelation through Jesus; the Son in His incarnate life, and the Holy Spirit as continuing the message of that life and realizing the divine-human sonship within the believers corporately because (first) individually.

We must bear in mind continually our limitations, indeed we are more cognizant now of the greatness of our ignorance; while the N.T. only tells us of the relations of God outwardly, and that towards man, we can but infer from that revelation which is threefold the inward relationship within the Godhead; this lay behind the record and the realization, as was felt when reflective thought began to deal with the subject.　As the personal Son or Word expressed and expresses the Thought or Reason of God, so the personal (Holy) Spirit expressed and expresses to man and in man the divine Will.

Towards man in his apprehension of revelation, the three modes of the Divine are realized to be distinct and verified as Father, Son, Spirit in daily experience, according to differing spheres of operation in a true sense personal. But no words can convey adequately our meaning, and no sufficient form of expression is attainable. When all our language is relative, and the mystery of God's inmost being so full of awe, we feel the wisdom of the word 'incomprehensible,' and, lest we say things unworthy or untrue, 'lay our hand upon our mouth.'

For not much is gained, we feel, by the imperfect analogies which were put forward in days later than the New Testament writings; and the best of human illustrations, social or individual, now are but chilly after the warm glow of intense personal realization of the threefold revelation, in the mutual abiding of man in God and God in man, in the interacting of spirit with Spirit, and that in Christ Jesus.

Surely the value of thoughts about the Holy Spirit in our day is measured by the personal worth of that personal experience constantly verified in the life, not only of God as loving Father, known as such through the Incarnate Son, but in that mode of being also which the N.T. calls the (Holy) Spirit; operating in and through us continually by divine indwelling, in guiding not compelling, requiring the personal response of faith, and moulding us to the pattern of Love and realizing progressively within us the life of sonship revealed in Christ.

Divine immanence would signify most of all with Paul this indwelling presence of the Spirit of God (or the Spirit of Christ) in the individual disciple; while with John it would seem to imply chiefly the continued spiritual presence of Jesus (or that of the Spirit of truth) in the Church of the faithful.

Ways of expression vary, re-interpretations, conscious or unconscious, go on according to the needs of each succeeding generation, under the Spirit's guidance, as the teaching of the Fourth Gospel claims. But the love of the Father changes not, the Logos ever reveals the Thought of God, the Spirit fulfils the Will, He is 'God working in us,' through many finite intelligences, indeed we ourselves on our tiny planet are His means; although the very thought of it subdues us with awe, yet it uplifts us with transcendent hope.

Conditioned as we are, we cannot really go beyond the N.T. doctrine of the self-witness of God through the Spirit in and through men; not indeed fresh outpouring, but more self-opening to the divine inflow is needed; more cherishing, too, of those homeliest graces which are, in the growing fulness of their exercise, His 'fruit.'

This belief in the Holy Spirit's activity we have found to have been an intense, a life-transforming power in the first age, but this belief just because of its vivid reality could not be defined in set phrases; and to-day the form of belief may be deemed orthodox, but may lack the glow and the produce of life.

We need in the present time as Churches and as individual disciples, with all our restless competition and our ceaseless controversies, more inwardness, more divine-human communion or interaction, more life ἐν τῷ πνεύματι.

To the writer this study, however broken and uneven, has, he hopes, quickened that life for himself; may this little work with all its defects stimulate others to further inquiry and to richer spiritual experience.

www.ingramcontent.com/pod-product-compliance
Ingram Content Group UK Ltd.
Pitfield, Milton Keynes, MK11 3LW, UK
UKHW042144280225
455719UK00001B/92